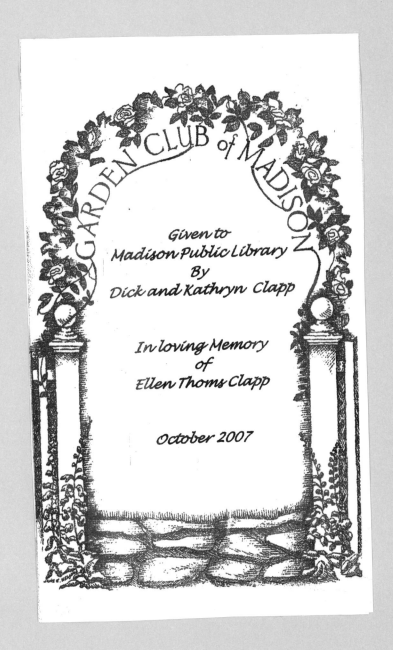

GARDEN CLUB of MADISON

Given to
Madison Public Library
By
Dick and Kathryn Clapp

In loving Memory
of
Ellen Thoms Clapp

October 2007

roses for the smaller garden

MARK MATTOCK

First published in the United States of America in 2001 by

Rizzoli International Publications, Inc.

300 Park Avenue South

New York, NY 10010

First published in Great Britain

in 2001 by

Quadrille Publishing Limited

Alhambra House

27-31 Charing Cross Road

London WC2H 0LS

ISBN 0-8478-2418-7

Library of Congress 2001092076

Printed in and bound in Germany

Contents

The rose story

The rose is one of the oldest flowering plants known to man and one of the most enduring and universal in its appeal. Although native to the northern hemisphere, roses are now grown in most countries of the world, including those in the southern hemisphere. Many books have been written about the history and legends of roses and all rosarians have fascinating stories to relate. The interest of this book, however, lies in the practical application of the knowledge achieved by the great gardeners and rose breeders of the past and, in particular, in the selection of types and varieties of rose for the modern gardener faced with limited space. It is fascinating to trace the process by which roses have evolved from their wild origins, first through gradual mutation and adaptation over the centuries and, more recently, through the ingenuity displayed by rose breeders in the techniques of hybridization to produce roses that meet the needs of today's small gardens.

Early history

Since before the beginnings of written history, the rose has featured in stories of adventure. Even before the formation of the great civilizations of the Near and Middle East, travelers were bringing specimens of this wondrous plant back from the East. Army mercenaries often included roses in their war booty, to grace the gardens of their masters.

We know the ancient Greeks cultivated roses. Coins from Rhodes, dating from 5000B.C., are imprinted with an image of a single, open flower, understood to be the rose. Theophrastus (ca.370–ca.286 B.C.), in his classification of all known plants of the time, writes of a rose having up to one hundred petals—perhaps *Rosa centifolia*—and of the five-petaled briar rose, still to be found today.

By the time of the Roman civilization, roses had become a symbol of wealth and luxury. Early Romans grew roses in specially constructed houses, heated to produce blooms during the winter. Roses were often used in the garlands presented to military heroes, and their petals strewn over the floors of banqueting halls. The ruins of Heraculaneum and Pompeii, left after the catastrophic volcanic eruption of Vesuvius in A.D.79, show villas surrounded by "peristyle" gardens of restricted size, very like our smaller gardens today. Boundary walls provided privacy, and central pools were often surrounded by flower beds in which roses would have grown, among other popular flowers. Roses are also depicted in frescoes found at Pompeii.

Pliny the Elder's Natural History contains references to roses that are thought to be forms of what we can now identify as *R. alba, R. canina, R. centifolia, R. damascena,* and *R. gallica.* After the fall of the Roman Empire, few, if any, references to these roses appeared in literature until King Childebert of France presented a rose garden to his queen in A.D.550, although we know roses were cultivated in the Byzantine Empire and Persia. Emperor Charlemagne is also credited with growing roses. But from the first century A.D., roses that survived in the West did so in the gardens of monasteries and large houses throughout Europe.

The distribution of the rose through the Mediterranean countries of southern and western Europe roughly parallels the spread of Islam, reaching Spain in the eighth century. Commerce and religion greatly influenced what Sappho (fl. ca.610–ca.580B.C.) called "the queen of flowers;" and the use of rose water in medicine (to mask the unpleasant smell of the potions used), as well as rose oil in perfume and cosmetics, and rose-leaf tea as an herbal drink, ensured its survival throughout the Middle Ages. During the twelfth and thirteenth centuries, the Crusaders introduced Europe to the rose varieties cultivated in Asia, when they brought back specimens from the Holy Land. Among those mentioned is *R. gallica* var. *officinalis*–still referred to as "the apothecary's rose" for its prominence in medicinal use as rose water.

By the early seventeenth century a number of different species and naturally occurring varieties, or sports, were being described in printed herbals in England and elsewhere in Europe. Most of these fell into the groups known as Gallicas, Damasks, and Albas, with their many-petaled, rosette-shaped blooms and shrubby growth. Some time later, another, similar group—the fragrant Centifolias—was developed by French and Dutch nurserymen, who had begun to sow seed and select the best seedlings to develop as new varieties. Around the same time, the European settlement of the New World introduced roses cultivated in Europe to North and South America, and the settlers sent back to Europe indigenous American species, including *Rosa virginiana* and *Rosa californica.* As far as we can tell, up to the eighteenth century, roses grown in gardens were planted in beds, trained against walls and fences and mixed with other plants—but never allowed to predominate.

▸ Rosa gallica *var.* officinalis, *"the apothecary's rose," was reputedly introduced by crusader Thibault IV to Provins in the Champagne region of France in the Middle Ages. The area became the commercial source of this medicinal rose, and remained so for six centuries.*

One of the earliest examples of a garden devoted to roses was at the palace of Malmaison, near Paris, created in 1799 for Napoleon's wife Josephine, to indulge her passion for roses. Her rosarian gardener, André Dupont, sowed seed from hips to make selections for new varieties. By the time of Josephine's death in 1814, the collection at Malmaison contained more than 250 varieties of rose planted in narrow beds, allowing all blooms to be examined at close quarters. Many varieties were recorded with remarkable accuracy and delicacy by the great court painter Pierre-Joseph Redouté. A number of his subjects can still be found in gardens today, though the size of the bushes and their limited season of bloom makes them unsuitable for the small contemporary garden.

The appearance of China roses

China roses, meanwhile, having reached southern Europe via the Silk Route (the trade route from the East through the Middle East to southern Europe), spread to northern Europe around the 1750s. We know that a clone of *Rosa x odorata* was grown at the Botanic Gardens at Kew in 1769, and *Rosa chinensis* var. *semperflorens* (Slater's Crimson China) arrived in Europe at this time. The remarkable characteristic of China roses, generally more sparse in growth than European roses, was their ability to bloom repeatedly through the summer, and this transformed the development of roses in Europe after the 1780s. The China rose was not difficult to propagate, and within quite a short time we find it recorded in France, Britain, and the United States.

The brothers Louis and Philippe Noisette, nurserymen in Paris and Charleston, South Carolina, assisted in the dissemination of the China rose. A wealthy rice planter, John Champney of Charleston, produced a hybrid between it and *Rosa moschata* which he named Champney's Pink Cluster. Seeds of this were gathered by Philippe Noisette and from

◀ Rosa *Adelaide d'Orléans, a* R. sempervirens *hybrid dating from 1826, is a typical once-flowering Rambler that is still grown today (colour engraving by Victor from a painting by Redouté.)*

the plants he raised, Philippe selected a white rose to send to his brother Louis in Paris. This is recognized to be the first Noisette rose, referred to by Redouté as *Rosa noisettiana*. Among its direct descendants we still grow the fragrant climbers Gloire de Dijon and Madame Alfred Carrière.

The tea-scented China roses were not hardy enough to be planted outdoors in northern climates, so during the nineteenth century they were grown in conservatories and crossed with hardier outdoor types like Hybrid Perpetuals, the first of the Modern roses. Not only did the Hybrid Perpetuals have upright growth and pointed buds, but many varieties were crimson, a colour absent in roses to date. This led eventually to the production of "Hybrid Teas."

In France the China rose had taken another direction and been developed into a group known as Tea-scented China roses, either for the resemblance of their scent to fresh tea leaves or because they were imported from the East in tea chests. The Tea roses share many characteristics with the China roses, being delicate in their growth and subject to frost in northern climates. Their lovely, dainty blooms often had pointed buds, and they were repeat blooming. Bourbon roses such as Madame Pierre Oger and Zéphirine Drouhin, the thornless rose, as well as Portland roses, all owe their existence to the Tea-scented China rose.

It was not until the mid-1800s that the legacy of early interest in the rose came to full fruition. The plantsmen of Victorian England were the first to carry out hybridization on any scale and, later in the century, breeding programmes in Europe and elsewhere developed the rose further, the exact directions being determined by the taste of the day and the public's shifting perceptions of rose beauty. At this time roses were bred almost entirely for their individual blooms (this was the age of the exhibition flower), with no regard for the plant's habit. But the first Hybrid Teas constituted a new kind of rose: short and upright growing, with high-pointed buds and flowers and large, glossy leaves—and they flowered repeatedly. Their habit of growth influenced the way roses started to be grown in gardens, in isolated "rose beds." This made sense aesthetically and practically, since they all needed similar culture, flowered at the same time, and were hard to mix attractively with other plants.

The evolution of modern roses

One of the features of the development of domestic architecture throughout the world since 1900 has been the advent of the smaller garden. In Britain, particularly, many town dwellers live in duplex ("semi-detached") and row houses, each with a narrow strip of garden in front and behind. Even in the United States, where abundant land has encouraged a pattern of large suburban lots, there has recently been a trend toward townhouse development, with relatively small garden space. It is no surprise to find the rose in one of its many forms decorating our confined outdoor living areas.

As the style and proportions of our gardens have been modified, so has the rose. By the early 1900s, when bedding roses included a few Hybrid Perpetuals and the early Hybrid Teas, purists in both the Old and the New World still believed roses should be strictly segregated in beds—mixed plantings being reserved for the informal country garden. So in the large town or country-house gardens of the affluent, pride of place in the center of sweeping lawns was given to formal rose beds, the same rose varieties grown and trained as standards being the only intrusions permitted in the beds.

The upright Hybrid Teas, with their pointed blooms, soon became so popular that they almost eclipsed the Old roses with their cupped blooms and bushy growth. The Hybrid Tea was subsequently slimmed down, making it appropriate for small gardens. The color range was also expanded from the previous palette of pinks, purples, and whites. In 1910 the first yellow rose appeared, followed by a range of warmer colors.

During the 1930s the Hybrid Tea was further refined to exaggerate its scrolled bud and pointed bloom. A milestone in its development was the introduction of the extraordinary variety known as Peace. In the immediate prewar years its appearance on the trial beds of its raisers, Antoine and François Meilland, in the south of France, excited much admiration. In addition to its large blooms and superb foliage, it had a vigor unheard of in a Bush rose. Propagating material was sent off to the raisers' distributors in Germany, Italy, and the United States so it could be offered to a wider public. But war intervened and before long Peace had appeared under the name of Gioia in Italy, Gloria Dei in Germany, and in France, the country of its origin, as Madame A. Meilland. At the end of the hostilities in 1945, with the inauguration of the United Nations, the wonder rose was officially launched under its most appropriate and universal name—Peace.

Alongside the development of Hybrid Teas, the Polyantha roses (grown previously in pots in conservatories) attracted the interest of rose breeders who developed them into the Polyantha pompoms. Resilient and hardy, with clusters of small Rambler-like flowers, they became the most fashionable bedding roses of the day. In the mid-1920s, Svend Poulsen, the master Danish rose hybridizer, crossed the Polyantha pompom with the Hybrid Tea, to produce a cluster-flowered rose with larger blooms. His dream of creating a new breed of bedding roses came to fruition in the 1930s with the release of his new varieties of "Poulsen roses," which he named after his daughters Ann, Kirsten, Karen, and Else. Once they began arriving from other sources, these roses were known as "Hybrid Polyanthas" and international rose breeders developed their blooms to resemble those of the Hybrid Teas more closely. By the 1950s, with the introduction of such great varieties as "Fashion" and "Spartan" from the United States, these roses differed so much from the earlier varieties that a new term, Floribunda, was universally adopted.

Hybrid Tea and Floribunda roses continued for a time to be regarded in the traditional way, as single-planting subjects. But the rise of the garden center in the United States and its spread to Europe in the 1960s tempted gardeners to try mixing bedding roses with the herbaceous plants suddenly available in containers. As a result, today's gardeners regard beds, borders, tubs, urns, and planters of all sizes as suitable arenas for roses.

◀ *The hundred-petaled rose,* Rosa centifolia, *was first referred to by Theophrastus, the "father of botany," around 300B.C. (painting by Redouté)*

Today's following for "miniature" roses started with *Rosa roulettii*, a tiny shrub 2in. (5cm.) tall, discovered in 1818 by Dr. Roulet, growing in pots on windowsills in a Swiss village. But it was not introduced commercially until 1922 and from such beginnings came a whole industry dealing with these tiny plants and their descendants; by 1977, there were more than 325 Miniature roses. Twenty years later, the miniaturized "patio" rose was introduced in Great Britain specifically for small gardens, a result of breeding short-growing Floribundas.

Climbing roses

Climbing roses have evolved, too. Until the middle of last century most Climbers were the result of mutations of current varieties of bedding rose, for example Climbing Crimson Glory. These, along with Ramblers like the famous Dorothy Perkins, a lax-growing type of Climber bred in 1901 by the large U.S. firm of Jackson Perkins, were midsummer flowering only; they spent the rest of the season producing new growth on which to flower the following year. But at almost the time of the Floribunda's emergence, in the mid-twentieth century, repeat blooming Climbers started to be introduced. The first was the well-known variety New Dawn, which has influenced the breeding of repeat blooming Climbers ever since. It is reputed to be a mutation of the tall, non-recurrent Rambler Dr. W. Van Fleet, resembling it in all respects other than flowering time.

Since the late 1980s, a new type of Climbing rose, known as the "patio climber" or "climbing miniature," has been bred for gardeners faced with the vertical aspect of boundaries in the small garden. Their foliage and blooms are in perfect scale with the plant's size—they are miniature-flowered as well as having small leaves and being short—and the blooms are borne in profusion from top to toe. The first, growing to 6ft. (2m.) tall and 3ft. (1m.) wide, was the bright, golden-yellow King Tut. They have proved excellent subjects for confined spaces, from fences to pillars.

Shrub roses

Modern Shrub and Hybrid Musk roses, with ideal repeat blooming characteristics, were developed in the twentieth century for the modern garden, where they may be used in mixed plantings or even hedges. Hybrid Musks bear large sprays of double flowers on tall, graceful growth, resembling a refined Floribunda. The best varieties were bred between 1900 and 1930 by the Reverend Mr. Pemberton of Essex, England. Modern Shrub roses are the result of crossing Hybrid Teas and Floribundas with a wide variety of different Species roses to produce a diverse class of Shrub roses with robust growth and flowers of modern appearance. The best known of these is the group developed in England by David Austin and known as English roses.

With the arrival of the successful Hybrid Tea roses in the early twentieth century, many of the Old rose varieties simply disappeared, and few were offered in growers' catalogs. However, in a concerted effort led by rosarian Graham Thomas, collectors searched out and preserved surviving examples of Old roses in their gardens. This revival of interest led teventually to their being exported around the world, from about 1950. The new English roses, introduced in the 1970s, combine the charms of these Old Garden roses with the merits of modern hybrids—full, many-petaled blooms, contemporary colors, glorious fragrances and, in many cases, disease resistance and a neat growing habit. With their more natural, informal appearance, they are well suited to mixed borders.

Meanwhile, the popularity of the shrubby growth and free flowering of the Floribundas, coupled with the demand for a ground-hugging plant to suppress annual weeds, influenced the recent introduction of a selection of spreading (Ground Cover) roses, the so-called Bodendecker roses, originating in Germany. These not only make excellent ground-cover plants but also are suitable for growing in containers. They evolved from *Rosa wichurana*, a Species of semi-prostrate habit, so they hug the ground, yet they have a strong affinity to Floribundas, with blooms down to ground level. They are marketed under the "County" and "Flower Carpet" series.

▸ *Striped* Rosa Mundi *started life as a sport of* Rosa gallica *var.* officinalis *and it was possible to find both forms of bloom on the same plant, flowering simultaneously.*

Classification of roses

There are, of course, hundreds of roses, all of which deserve much more space than we can allot either in this book or in the garden. However, their influence is important in the development of our Modern Garden roses. The definition of rose types that follows is the result of much deliberation by the World Federation of Rose Societies to clarify what may seem to be a bewildering family.

Modern Garden roses

These are roses of hybrid origin that bear no strong resemblance to wild (species) roses and were not included in any classification in general use before the introduction of Hybrid Tea roses. Within this group are Non-climbing and Climbing types.

Non-climbing Modern Garden roses
Plants with self-supporting stems. These roses are subdivided into recurrent blooming roses, whose flowering season is long or with a marked resurgence later, and nonrecurrent blooming roses, whose flowering season is limited to spring or summer with, at best, only occasional blooms in the fall. By far the bigger group are the non-climbing, recurrent blooming roses, which are divided into the following categories:

Shrub roses are defined as plants that are usually taller and/or possibly wider than Bush roses and are particularly suitable for use as specimen plants. Ground Cover roses fall within this category.

Bush roses are varieties of moderate height that are particularly suitable for cultivation in groups.

Hybrid Tea roses usually have flowers of medium to large size; the petals of double and semi-double varieties overlap to form a conical, ovoid, or other symmetrical center, and those of single varieties are large and form a shapely bud. They lend themselves to being cut as individual flowers (with or without side buds) on a long stem.

Floribunda roses are distinguished primarily by a mass of flowers produced in trusses, in clusters, or on many stems. They may be single, semi-double, or double.

Polyantha roses have small double flowers, usually of rosette form, borne in large clusters, and distinctive foliage, the leaflets being smaller than those of Floribunda roses.

Miniature roses have miniature flowers, foliage, and growth.

Climbing Modern Garden roses are defined as climbing or rambling plants with long sprawling or arching stems requiring support. Again they are subdivided into nonrepeating Climbing roses, whose flowering season is limited to spring or summer with, at best, only occasional blooms in the fall, and recurrent-flowering Climbing roses, whose flowering season is long or has a marked resurgence later. Within both groups of Climbing rose are:

Ramblers, climbing roses with lax stems.

Climbers, with stiffer stems than Ramblers.

Climbing miniatures or patio climbers with very small flowers and foliage.

Each ultimate class may be further divided into double (normally having more than 20 petals), semi-double (8–20 petals), and single-flowered (fewer than 8 petals).

Old Garden roses

This term refers to roses that were already well established in classifications in common use before the introduction of Hybrid Tea roses. These classes were based largely on presumed genetic and botanical affinities and, in general, do not fit into the modern classification which is based mainly on garden use. Again, they are divided into Non-climbing and Climbing types.

Non-Climbing Old Garden roses have self-supporting stems and include the following types:

Alba Roses displaying the influence of *Rosa alba*.

Bourbon Roses displaying the influence of *Rosa x bourboniana*, supposedly a hybrid between the China rose and Autumn Damask.

Boursault Roses supposedly displaying the influence of *Rosa chinensis* and *Rosa pendulina*.

China Roses displaying the influence of *Rosa chinensis*.

Damask Roses displaying the influence of *Rosa damascena*.

Gallica Roses displaying the influence of *Rosa gallica*.

Hybrid perpetual Roses usually interbreeding Bourbon roses with China or Damask roses.

Moss Roses with mossy outgrowth on sepals and/or pedicels.

Portland Roses allied to "Duchess of Portland" (a hybrid), suggesting the influence of China and Damask roses.

Provence (Centifolia) Roses displaying the influence of *Rosa centifolia*.

Sweet briar Roses displaying the influence of *Rosa eglanteria* (syn. *R. rubiginosa*).

Tea roses Roses displaying the influence of *Rosa x odorata*, supposedly a hybrid between *Rosa chinensis* and *Rosa gigantea*.

Climbing Old Garden roses are climbing or rambling plants with long sprawling or arching stems normally requiring support. They divide as follows:

Ayrshire Roses displaying the influence of *Rosa arvensis*.

Boursault Roses supposedly displaying the influence of *Rosa chinensis* and *Rosa pendulina*.

Climbing Tea Climbing roses with flowers similar to those of Tea roses.

Noisette Roses displaying the influence of *Rosa x noisettiana*, supposedly a hybrid between *Rosa chinensis* and *Rosa moschata*.

Sempervirens Roses displaying the influence of *Rosa sempervirens*.

Wild roses

These include Species roses and their varieties or hybrids (either single- or double-flowered) which bear a strong resemblance to the species. They are divided into Non-climbing and Climbing types, defined as before.

Roses in the small garden

Roses are among the easiest, and most amenable, plants to grow. With good feeding and reasonable care and attention, they will thrive in almost any soil and give years of enjoyment. No matter how small your garden, or how irregular the boundaries, whether you are hemmed in by walls, fences, or hedges, there is a rose for every aspect, bringing color throughout the summer months. If you have an awkward corner, a Shrub rose will bring interest to it, and if you wish to add height to a flower bed, a standard rose could be the solution. Climbing roses provide vertical decoration at and above eye level, while some of the old Ramblers, no longer planted on walls and fences because their flowering season is so short, may be grown to twine through old trees.

Choosing roses for your garden

▲ Climbing rose Compassion, trained on a dividing trellis and flowering profusely, frames the picture presented by the geometric shapes of the clipped box and the mixed border featuring the Floribunda, Iceberg, a reliable old favorite.

Whether you are thinking about planting a single specimen rose or a quantity to group together, you need to be sure that you have chosen correctly. First ask yourself some pertinent questions about what you want the rose(s) to do.

Is it to grow against a wall or fence? Which direction will it face? If your rose is to face a northern or eastern aspect, it will be in shade for a greater part of the day, so you will need to select a free-flowering variety, like pale pink Compassion or champagne-colored Penny Lane, which bloom well even in shade. What color flowers do you prefer? You know what your favorite color is, but will this be the right color to plant against a brick or stone wall or a painted wooden fence? Will it complement companion plants or, if container grown, the terracotta color of clay pots? Where roses are grown on a terrace or patio adjacent to the house you may also want to bear in mind the color scheme of the living area or even of the draperies that frame it when viewed through the windows. How big is the wall to be covered? You will need to look up the plant's mature height and, for a high wall, choose a tall-growing variety such as Summer Wine or Madame Alfred Carrière.

Is the rose to plant in a mixed border or an island bed? How will you choose between large-flowered (Hybrid Tea) roses, cluster-flowered roses (Floribundas)—both of them upright growing—or bushy Shrub roses? What color are the plants next to the rose? How tall need it grow to fit into the overall "picture?" It is important to find out the mature height of your proposed planting and never a good idea to plant a tall, leggy variety at the edge of a much-used path, though it could have a role at the back of a border. The same, of course, applies to the spread of a broad shrub, as you do not want to have to brush against soggy foliage in wet weather. But in the middle of a bed, Shrub roses such as Hansaland or Ballerina could look good. Do you want to be able to cut blooms for indoors? If so, what is the color scheme of your furnishings? The best roses for cutting are long, smooth-stemmed varieties.

Roses are excellent subjects to grow alongside other garden plants, and it is important to exploit the potential of mixing different flower shapes and textures. Suitable companions are discussed in more detail later in the chapter (see page 46). Having decided on the type of rose, the color of its bloom and foliage, and the overall size of the plant, it is now time to begin the enjoyable task of selecting the exact variety, or varieties, for your garden.

Selecting for confined spaces

In a small area any plant must pay its rent by giving good returns for the space allotted to it, and this is particularly true of roses. It is very easy to look at pictures of beautiful roses and to make up your mind that you must have such charmers

▾ *This mixed border on the boundary features a happy use of the Rambling rose Albéric Barbier, together with roses and other seasonal shrubs. Although a Rambler is not the best choice for a small garden, here it gives height where it is most needed.*

as, say, Nevada or Frühlingsgold (both Shrub roses). The simplicity of their large, single, open flowers can easily win you over, until you find that they will both grow to some 8ft. (2.5m.) and may dwarf anything else you wish to plant in your restricted border. Besides this, neither of them will give you the continuity of bloom that a smaller garden demands.

This does not mean, of course, that in a small garden you are destined to grow only the shorter Floribundas, known as "patio" roses. But you may wish to give preference to roses of a neat habit, with controlled vigor, that will not outgrow their allocated space. It also makes sense to select roses with good disease resistance, as enclosed, urban sites are often airless and foster fungal growth such as mildew, as well as attracting aphids. In terms of clothing walls and fences, you would generally choose Climbers or "patio climbers" over Ramblers, which have too lax and untidy a habit, in addition to blooming only once. Perhaps the most important quality is a long flowering time, or repeat flowering, because when not in bloom, roses may be of limited interest in the garden. Choosing roses that produce hips is another way of extending interest into the fall; bear in mind that most of these will be single-flowered rather than double-flowered.

The more ornamental characteristics a rose has, the stronger its claim for inclusion in the smaller garden. A rose with attractive foliage, as well as beautiful blooms, will make more of a contribution when not in flower. Some Hybrid Tea roses, such as Royal William and Just Joey, have particularly attractive bronze-red juvenile foliage, while *Rosa glauca* (*R. rubrifolia*) has glorious mauve-gray leaves which complement perfectly its single pink flowers and autumnal hips. Roses with good scent add an appealing quality to an individual's experience of a small garden, especially on a

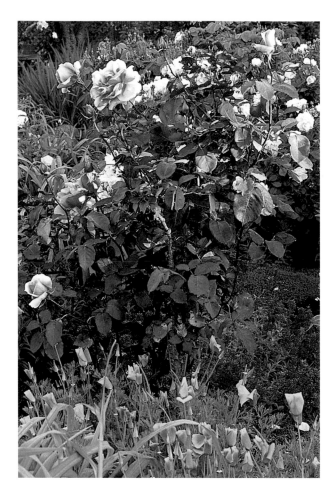

▲ *The Hybrid Tea rose Just Joey was voted "the world's favorite rose" at an international rose convention held in New Zealand in 1994. In this mixed bed it has vividly colored lavender and annual eschscholzias at its feet.*

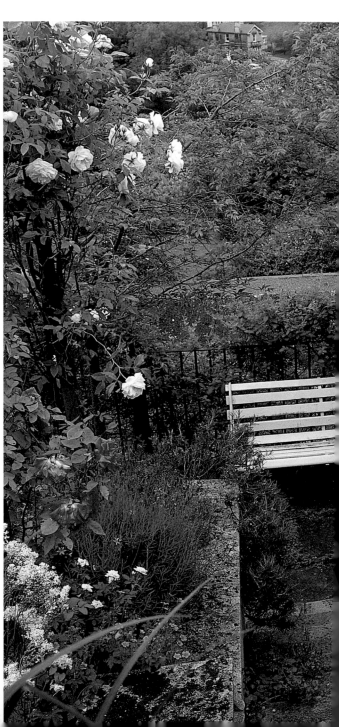

summer evening, as scents tend to be distilled in confined spaces. So, wherever possible, try to choose a fragrant rose over one that has no scent. There is no substance to the claims that "modern roses have lost their smell;" writers in the 1880s were complaining about much the same thing, and no doubt others will do so in the future, but contemporary rose breeders are all too conscious of retaining and enhancing this desirable characteristic whenever they can.

▲ *The apothecary's rose,* Rosa gallica *var.* officinalis, *can grow to 5ft. (1.5m.) in height but in this narrow bed it is deliberately kept low by pruning out all the old wood immediately after blooming.*

◂ *Bourbon rose Zéphirine Drouhin is trained as a pillar to contrast with the white climbing rose, both of which add height to the beds on either side of the steps, while helping to screen the unexceptional view beyond the garden.*

Purchasing your roses

Once you have chosen the roses you wish to plant it is important, first of all, to choose a good supplier. Talk to other gardeners, and send off for mail-order catalogs, because an informative catalog can reveal much about the nursery. Most reputable suppliers give guarantees and offer a reliable service, but it still makes sense to shop around. If you wish to see a particular rose variety "in the flesh" before you consider buying it, you should visit local flower shows and open gardens, as well as seeing what is available at your local garden center or nursery.

Roses can be purchased in several different forms: what you choose will depend on availability and season.

▲ The purple-gray foliage and hips of Rosa glauca *can be used to great effect to enhance the color of other flowering subjects. It is seen here with late summer-flowering shrubby mallow* (Lavatera olba rosea).

▶ In this semi-formal design, symmetrically placed roses soften and embellish the layout. The soft color of Climbing rose New Dawn frames the view while Hybrid Musk roses flank the steps and pink Hybrid Teas furnish the beds.

Bare-rooted Nursery-fresh plants, dug from the rose fields, where they have been grafted onto briar "understocks," are sold bare-rooted, either by mail order or collected direct from the nursery, in the traditional planting season, when the plants are in a dormant state during the winter months.

Containerized Having been propagated and grown in the nursery beds, these roses have been taken up and replanted into pots so that they may be offered for sale in garden centers throughout the year. Some nurseries even prepare roses for sale by propagating them in pots on their own roots.

Prepackaged These roses, nursery grown, are lifted early in the season, sometimes before they are dormant, and sold in plastic packages, after being coated with wax preservative to enable them to withstand temperatures encountered inside the stores. Since many stores are kept too hot for the health of roses, it may be best to avoid buying them this way.

Rose awards

So universal is a love of the rose that almost all countries have a society devoted to its development and promotion. Most of these societies belong to The World Federation of Rose Societies, and all distribute their publications. Among their main activities are testing new varieties under local conditions and rewarding the best with awards and recommendations. Seeing which roses receive awards may make your choice of varieties easier. The awards are listed in the book within the description of each profiled rose. An explanation of the abbreviations used is given below:

AARS   All-American Rose Selection

ARS   American Rose Society

ADR   Anerkannte Deutsche Rose

HE   Harry Edland medal for best scented rose seedling of the year

PIT   President's International Trophy for best new seedling rose of the year

RNRS   Royal National Rose Society

TGC   Trial Ground Certificate

JMMM   James Mason Memorial Medal for a rose which has given particular pleasure to rose lovers. (The actor was an enthusiastic rose grower.)

Planning rose beds and borders

The shape, size, and position of beds and borders will depend to a great extent on the dimensions and layout of your garden, as well as its style. Your layout might demand the open space of a lawn, with borders against the boundaries, backed by a wall or fence; or you may have a paved area in which island beds will find a setting. You may wish to create a formal look, with symmetrical borders containing a fairly regimented planting of neat, compact plants, or you may prefer the informality of an asymmetric bed which, through the careful placing of plants of different shapes, sizes, and colors, has a balance of its own.

Planting an island bed

The term island bed, or "island," refers to a planted area in your garden which will be viewed from every side—a path, surrounding lawn, or a paved area—so the planting has to look good all around. The idea of island beds started with formal beds cut out in geometric shapes in the lawns of nineteenth-century gardens. The more gardeners one employed, the more intricate the shape of the bed could be; all the edging was laborious and time-consuming. If you are planning a new island bed, keep the outline simple—whether circular, elliptical, square, or rectangular—to cut down on the

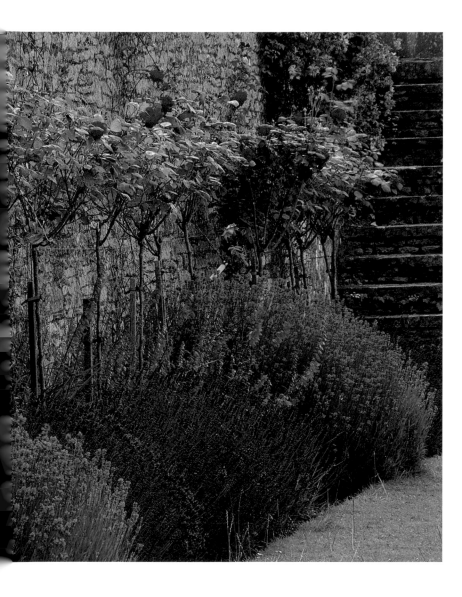

work involved. Its dimensions will, of course, be governed by the site, but if you have a choice, make sure the relevant regular planting distances (seee page 150) fit the bed exactly. Try not to make an island too deep or too wide, because when working among the roses you will want to reach the middle of the bed without difficulty. If the bed has to be deep or wide, however, make access easier by laying carefully sited stepping-stones.

Besides keeping the edge of the lawn trimmed, nineteenth-century fashion also decreed that beds be edged with a low hedge, usually box (*Buxus sempervirens*) or lavender (*Lavandula*). These edged beds still exist in gardens of traditional formal design, but new ideas have also developed out of them. We now see mixed beds, edged with modern "patio" roses—Floribundas such as Festival, Mandarin, or Queen Mother, or large Miniatures up to 18in. (45cm.) in height, like Baby Masquerade or Royal Salute. The spreading Ground Cover varieties such as Avon and Kent are also used to edge beds. Using Ground Cover roses to fill awkward corners of an irregularly shaped island will help to prevent visitors or the mailman from taking a short cut across an empty corner of the bed. When paths surround the island and an edging is not used, leave at least 18in. (45cm.) between the front row of roses and the edge of the path. Avoid planting wide-spreading bedding varieties near the edge, as they would eventually overhang the path or lawn, causing clothing to be caught by a thorny branch.

The smaller your garden, the less likely you are to keep your island bed for bedding roses only. Low-growing spring-flowering plants, including bulbs, can be planted at the foot of roses and provide interest in another season. When planning the overall shape of your planting and looking for taller subjects, bear in mind that most of the Old Garden roses bloom for only a short midsummer season on the previous season's growth, and do not lend themselves to being restrained by pruning. However, Modern Shrub roses, including English roses, bloom on the current year's growth and may therefore be pruned to create the shape you want.

If you are mixing types of rose—for example, bedding roses such as Floribundas and Hybrid Teas with the more

▲ Standard roses, with superb lavenders at their feet, have been planted closer together than normal and used instead of climbers to furnish a wall in this restrained, contemporary planting scheme.

◄ In an original twist on the idea of edging beds with low box hedges, this topiary feature cut into geometric shapes uses Rosa glauca as an attractive infill. The small blooms will be followed by a fine crop of brilliant red hips.

vigorous Shrub roses—remember that they each require different planting distances, and planting in well-ordered rows may be impossible. Include as many repeat-blooming roses as you can to ensure that the display is not limited to a few weeks in early summer. It is important to aim for an overall balance when designing your planting, so bear this in mind when you mark out the planting positions. You may not wish to present an even bank of color, in which case clumps of different shape can be achieved by varying the selection of varieties. Perfect balance can, in any case, be boring to the eye, and an asymmetric design may bring more interest to your planting. For example, you may set the tallest "focal point" plant deliberately off-center to prevent a planting from looking like a predictable and regimented pyramid.

When selecting subjects for island beds, make sure that what you choose is in proportion to the size and shape of the bed and to any other plants you are using in the bed or in the background. You would not plant big Shrub roses in a small bed or even a small garden, however beautiful their blooms,

as they would be out of proportion. Standard roses and taller varieties can be included if you wish to "lift" an otherwise flat bed, but they need careful siting (see page 34). As a general guideline, plant the low-growing "patio" roses and Ground Cover roses at the front and the taller, more upright Hybrid Tea and Floribunda varieties in the middle of your island. Follow the planting distances on page 150 to ensure your selected roses will not obscure those growing behind them.

Roses in the mixed border

Most borders are intended to be seen from the front or sides, with paths, lawns, or paved areas in front and, usually, a taller screen at the back. This screen, which may take the form of a wall, fence, or hedge, will provide a background against which shorter subjects will be seen. Informality is easier to achieve in a border than an island bed. Many of today's mixed borders have evolved from the concept of the old herbaceous borders, which involved much work in weeding, dividing, and replanting perennials at regular intervals. Some still contain several of the old favorite clump-forming herbaceous perennials which make classic combinations with Shrub roses. Later in the chapter, subjects for planting alongside your roses are discussed in detail (see page 46).

In a rose border there is scope, provided the dimensions allow, to plant a host of different types of rose. Shapes, colors, and sizes can be blended for an overall effect, or they may be deliberately contrasted for more impact. As we have seen, it is important to plan for interest through the seasons. Early-blooming varieties such as Canary Bird, a fine yellow briar rose, could start the season. At 5ft. (1.5m.) high, it is not too large for the smaller garden, and its foliage is ornamental throughout the summer. Such a rose will provide a dainty companion to the splash of color to follow, from the early summer-blooming Shrub roses, the summer and autumn repeat-blooming varieties of Floribunda and Hybrid Tea roses, as well as the "patio" and ground-hugging varieties—not forgetting the repeat-blooming Shrub roses which will carry your display through to autumn. If space allows, you could include some summer-flowering Species roses and hybrids which bear ornamental hips, like *Rosa*

▼ Demonstrating how roses of all types contribute to the mixed border, Shrub rose R. gallica 'Charles de Mills' and English rose Heritage with Hybrid Tea Silver Jubilee are greatly enhanced by herbaceous perennials (below left).

▼ The Bourbon rose Zéphirine Drouhin can be grown as a freestanding shrub in a bed or as a Climbing rose to cover a wall (below right).

◀ *Modern Shrub rose Ballerina,*
seen here repeated through a bed
with gypsophila and violas,
offers a long season of interest.
Its apple-blossom pink blooms
continue until the first frosts,
after which it is smothered with
clusters of tiny beadlike hips.

'Geranium' (a *R. moyesii* selection), or one of the Rugosas or their hybrids, which will provide late-fall fruit and may show color into winter if the birds leave the hips for you.

How you arrange the different varieties depends on the effect you wish to achieve. For example, if space permits, Hybrid Musk roses such as Cornelia provide attractive arching shapes and look superb when surrounded, or fronted, by Ground Cover roses such as Sommermarchen, Avon, or Pink Bassimo. A more upright variety like Robusta will be well set off by a bushy Floribunda such as Anna Livia. If your border is backed by a wall, plant a Climbing rose against it for background interest; Compassion would complement Cornelia, Golden Showers would contrast effectively with Robusta. If you do not have a fence or wall to support climbers, a planting of *Rosa moyesii* would provide taller tracery as background.

The size of the border will have a bearing on the shape you wish your roses to have when seen sideways from the house. The larger the border, the greater should be the size of the "clumps" of roses used, and repeating the clumps will create a sense of balance. When planting more than one of a variety, use uneven numbers for the most amenable shape. Clumps of rosebushes help break up straight lines and escape the constraints imposed by rigidly defined boundaries, especially in long, narrow gardens. Use standard roses to provide extra height or give a broken line to the middle of a border, but if you wish to avoid the formality of a line of standards, grow shorter Climbing roses on pillars or obelisks to provide vertical interest. Choose a "patio" rose or a more restrained Climber—such as Altissimo, Grand Hotel, or Handel. Space nonrepeating varieties among repeat-blooming subjects so whole areas are not left blank in the fall.

Using Shrub roses

When the Hybrid Teas and Floribunda roses heralded the arrival of the more manageable bedding roses, the previously popular once-blooming Shrub roses lost their importance in the smaller garden. But in recent years interest in these shrubby roses has grown, especially as Modern Shrub roses now have repeat blooming bred into them. Some varieties may be used successfully as boundary hedges and garden dividers (see page 41), but there are other parts of the small, contemporary garden that cry out for the use of Shrub roses. It is also important to note that, from time to time, roses have been introduced which defy classification but which, due to their appearance and habit of growth, have been marketed under the title of Modern Shrub roses. They are, in the main, repeat-flowering varieties which merely require trimming to size and shape each year.

Some of the Old Garden roses can be grown singly for their display in even the smallest border, although they have only a short blooming season. Moss rose Nuits de Young, a deep purplish maroon, is smaller than Common Moss, and introduces a color unusual in the modern garden. *Rosa gallica* var. *versicolor*, better known as Rosa Mundi, the striped rose of ancient times, is well worth the limited space it takes up; keep it in trim by removing the old flowering shoots each fall. Many of the older hybrid Rugosas are too large for a confined space, but Frau Dagmar Hastrup (see page 133), is more restrained in stature and is useful as a hedge or as a specimen plant in the mixed border. The same applies to the newer hybrid Rugosas from Germany, like Robusta and The Compass. Other old favorites include Portland roses, such as De Rescht and Jacques Cartier, which combine the charm of Old Garden roses—too big for a limited space—with amenable size and the virtue of repeat blooming. When planting a Shrub rose, note its expected mature height. A short grower (up to 3ft. [1m.] tall) needs less space around it than one of medium stature (see Planting Distances, page 150). Plant a group of a single variety closer than this, to grow into each other and make a solid clump.

Rose breeders have made great strides in recent years. The idea of crossing some Old Garden roses with Modern Hybrid Teas and Floribundas originated with David Austin of Shropshire, England, who named his brilliant selection "English roses." There are many excellent varieties to choose from, combining most of the outstanding characteristics of Old and Modern roses. The full, many-petaled blooms, soft colors, and fragrance of the Old roses have been partnered by new colors, repeat-blooming, and different styles of growth. If some are too tall to control as border plants, you could train them as pillar roses or grow them against a fence. The best varieties for this are Gertrude Jekyll (one of the best scented roses of all time), Graham Thomas, and The Pilgrim.

Using Miniature and patio roses

A thriving pot rose industry has arisen in Europe in recent years. The important Danish rose-breeding firm, Poulsen (of Hybrid Polyantha fame) is producing these pot roses by the million under the trade names of "Parade" and "Hit" roses, with such varieties as "Pink Hit," "Sun Hit," and "Velvet Hit." In the U.K. this has led to the development of a more robust-growing outdoor group, the "patio" roses, greatly influenced by the cluster-flowered roses from which they were selected. These bushes quickly became popular, especially for small gardens. Only 18–20in. (45–50cm.) tall, they can be planted in containers, making them ideal for use on terraces and patios, as well as at the front of small mixed borders.

▲ Patio roses such as Festival (voted Rose of the Year 1994) are selections from the shorter-growing Floribundas. They make ideal subjects for confined spaces, for edging beds, and for growing in containers.

◄ Lax-growing Hybrid Musk roses, including Buff Beauty, with its soft coloring, make excellent subjects for the mixed border in conjunction with herbaceous perennials and other ornamental trees and shrubs.

Using Ground Cover roses

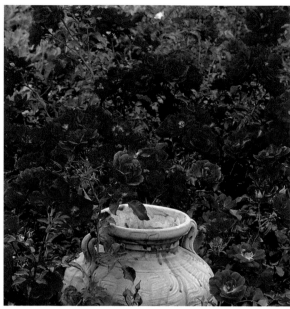

▲ The County series are superb ground-hugging roses which bloom from early summer until the frosts of late fall. Kent, seen above, has won many international awards and is ideal for small borders.

▲ Flower Carpet (above right) is a brilliant ground-covering rose. It was highly promoted throughout the world in the 1990s and is proving to be extremely disease-resistant.

Whatever the name given to these ground-hugging, sprawling shrubs, they offer great value when used in the small garden. The spreading habit of some of these lax-growing rose varieties still shows a strong affinity to *Rosa wichurana*, a trailing white, scented species introduced from Japan in 1860 which gave rise to the range of Climbing roses known as the Ramblers. It was almost a century before their ground-hugging habit was used by breeders in the production of a new race of ground cover roses. The Fairy, introduced in 1932, is probably the best known survivor of this early type and it has been much used in breeding since.

At the start of the latter half of the twentieth century, two distinct types of ground-covering rose emerged and were quickly recognized for their worth by the landscaping sector of the horticultural industry. Big bushy plants arrived from the Netherlands, Denmark, and France, while another wide-spreading, prostrate grower, typified by Kordes' Gamebird series, came from Germany. These are the joint precursors of today's Ground Cover roses.

A decade or so after the appearance of these large, sprawling, but short-flowering varieties, exciting things began to happen. Through the use of the repeat blooming, cluster-flowered (Floribunda) varieties in their breeding, low-growing ground-hugging plants often of only 3ft. (1m.) across were produced and introduced as Ground Cover roses. Planted at 3ft. (1m.) apart, these sprawling bedding roses soon became popular for planting in both beds and borders, where they completely covered the ground, suppressing annual weeds. The attractive hummocks they produce are especially useful in small gardens, where they flower throughout summer and autumn until the first frosts.

The need to differentiate these exciting modern roses from their sprawling forebears became clear as their many contemporary uses made themselves apparent. Marketing solved the problem. One selection, originating from varieties with common characteristics produced by the great hybridizers, Kordes in Germany and Poulsen in Denmark, was promoted in Britain under the "family" name of The County Series, each variety named after a county in Britain. Other groups include the Flower Carpet series, originating in Germany, which has been successful worldwide. Much has been written about the original vivid colored variety, now called Pink Flower Carpet, especially of its disease-resistant foliage. White Flower Carpet (see page 123), my own favorite, is one of the best white scented bedding roses grown today. Other plant breeders, too, have been busy with this type of rose: Warner's Pathfinder is an eye-catching variety whose brilliant vermilion-scarlet blooms are borne in profusion on typical ground-hugging growth.

Besides fulfilling their original use, many of these roses were also budded onto stems to make attractive weeping standards (see page 34), especially those with abundant lax stems and good foliage, such as Avon, Aspen, and Hertfordshire. The ground-hugging characteristics of these roses can also be put to good use at the edge of a retaining wall, or close to the edge of a pool, where the plant's beauty will be reflected in the water. Ground-covering roses such as those in The County Series are also ideal in small beds, on banks, and as the edging for mixed shrub borders. Planted to within 2ft. (60cm.) of the edge of a border, they will smother the soil surface and provide a perfect finish to a flowerbed.

▲ The Fairy set standards by which more recent Ground Cover varieties are measured. The dainty sprays of tiny, soft pink double blooms are heaped layer upon graceful layer into a hummock-like shrub, seen here in a small bed with phlox and campanulas.

◀ *Roses of pliant growth are budded onto tall-stemmed briars to produce weeping standards that display cascades of massed blooms in midsummer. Here a white form of Dorothy Perkins is used to line a garden path.*

Using standard roses

In Tenniel's famous illustrations for the children's classic *Alice's Adventures in Wonderland*, the roses shown in the Queen of Hearts' garden are depicted as standards—that is, bush roses grafted on clear stems, bringing the blooms of even the shortest growers up to eye level. The varieties offered for sale as standards at nurseries and garden centers tend to be the most popular roses of a well-shaped, compact habit. They may be (but are not necessarily) large-flowered or even cluster-flowered varieties; "patio" roses, Shrub roses, and Ground Cover varieties may also be grown as standards to make simple accents in a garden. Avoid varieties that are tall, leggy or even straggly, because the resultant standard plant will be ungainly. The stem of half-standards, used less often but in the same way, are usually 2ft. (60cm.) tall, and those of full standards are 3ft. (1m.).

Weeping standards are budded even higher, at 5ft. (1.5m.) above ground level, and are another excellent means of adding height to a bed of uniformly growing bedding roses. The cascade of blooms hides the stake or any ugly infrastructure. Budding the stem with a lax-growing variety produces a weeping standard; these are most attractive, though they may need extra care and attention. Where Ramblers are used, remember that they are usually summer-flowering varieties, and, when pruning, you must leave the new growth to flower in the following year. Older growth which has already flowered may be removed, but only if such drastic action does not leave a gaping hole in the outline of the head. Some nurseries now offer weeping standards of the prostrate-growing Ground Cover varieties. They promise to be excellent additions to the small rose garden, blooming as they do for a much longer season than the old Ramblers. It is possible to train weeping standards over a metal frame, but I prefer the production of a natural weeping habit.

There is little difference in planting procedure between standard and Bush roses, except that standards will need to be staked. Drive a stake into the ground to support the trunk before planting a standard (to avoid damaging the roots), with the top of the stake to come just below the lowest branches. Some stems may produce suckers between the budding point and ground level. These are natural shoots from the rootstock which should not be left to mature. Remove by rubbing off the juvenile bud when it appears.

A good basic rule of planning and planting is to make sure the plant is in balance with its neighbors. Standard roses should not be too close to other standards (6–9ft. [2–3m.] is a good distance), though the pairing or repetition of standards throughout a bed gives it a structural symmetry. Any underplanting should also be in proportion; so with a standard Peace, for example, use other roses that are not too tall-growing, as you do not want to detract from the focal effect of the standard. Do not plant standard roses in the path of an icy draft (from a gap in a wall, fence, or hedge, for example); being higher up makes them vulnerable to cold, and in very exposed areas some protection may be needed.

When pruning standards (Bush and Floribunda varieties), if you wish to ensure that the new season's growth will make a well-balanced shape, study the dormant growth buds and their position after pruning. Cutting to an outward-pointing "eye" ensures that new growth will not clog up the center of the bushy head, thus allowing good air circulation. To avoid wind damage during the winter, cut longer shoots back by half before the onset of hard weather.

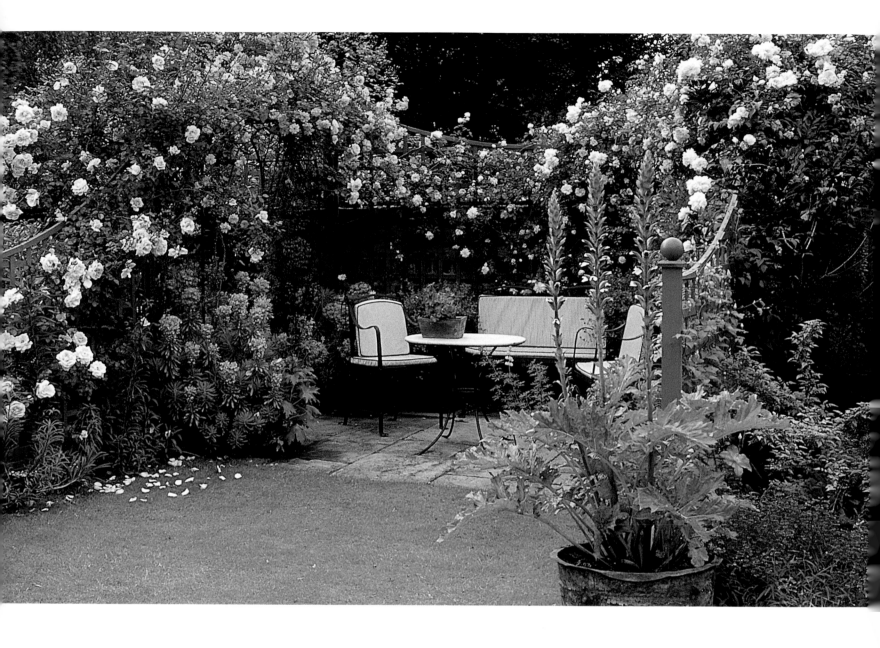

Climbing roses on walls and fences

▲ Fragrance fills the air and "walls" of colorful Climbing roses, among them New Dawn, surround and enclose this paved seating area at the far end of a small garden.

In small town gardens with high boundaries, where there is more vertical than horizontal space, Climbing roses are invaluable. They are equally useful to cover unattractive close-boarded fences as to cover boundary walls and house walls. There are many Climbing roses to choose from, suitable for all aspects, wall sizes, and situations. Well before Modern roses came on the scene, Climbers were used to clothe house walls, boundary walls, and the dividing walls found within some gardens as screens and windbreaks.

Climbing roses do not have a natural habit of climbing, being neither twining by nature nor equipped with tendrils to support them, as are other climbers. They therefore need to be attached to a firm frame made by fixing taut wires or trellis to the support, be it a wall, fence or the house. If you want good wall coverage, it is important to train the basal shoots of Climbers out horizontally and to choose a variety that produces plenty of lateral shoots as well as being able to reach to the top of a fence. Good small-garden varieties with many lateral shoots include Compassion, Penny Lane, Summer Wine, New Dawn, and Altissimo.

Bending the lower branches constricts the flow of sap, which ensures that foliage and flowers are generated from the base of the plant, whereas a Climbing rose trained vertically will often produce top growth only, leaving bare stems at eye level. Unless the lateral shoots are properly secured they can become quite unmanageable. Attach plastic-covered or galvanized wires to vine eyes or masonry nails screwed into the wall or fence; the wires should be strained tight and should stand about 2in. (5cm.) proud of the wall to allow air circulation. The branches of the rose can then be attached by ties of soft brown fillis twine rather than with wires or plastic string which will eventually "strangle" the shoots and therefore weaken the rose. When the strings disintegrate through age, they will simply need replacing with new ties. Wooden trellis panels, either attached to a wall or making a freestanding screen, can also be used as a support for Climbing roses. Fix the branches to the outside of the trellis, so that it is easy to take the Climber down for pruning or retraining.

Not all varieties will be suitable for every situation that calls for a Climbing rose. Recommendations for which Climbers to grow where can be found on page 161. Many lists show varieties as being suitable for growing on shady northern aspects, which really means that they are hardy enough to tolerate the conditions experienced in such a situation. No rose likes to be grown in total shade, as witnessed by the number of spindly, half-starved specimens seen struggling for existence in dark passages and other shady situations. But there may be a case for planting a Climber on a northwest-facing wall or a favored east-facing wall where it gets just enough sunlight to encourage bloom, especially if you choose the most free-flowering varieties. Climbing rose Mermaid is often recommended for walls in shade, but bear in mind that it may be cut to the ground by a harsh northeasterly wind. On the other hand, given some protection, Mermaid can reach enormous proportions, so bear this in mind when searching for a favored position for this variety of rose.

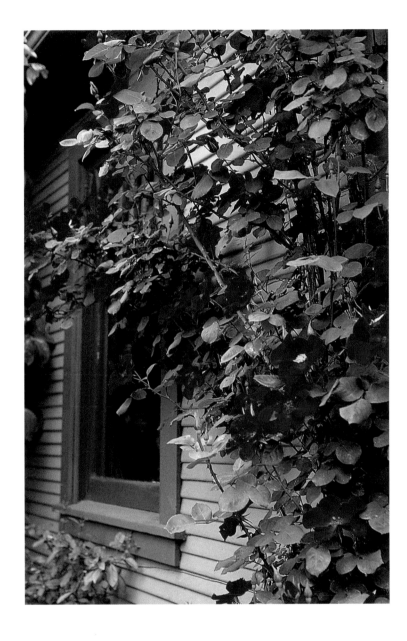

The most important criteria for even dappled shade would be the extraordinary freedom of bloom found in almost all of the recently-bred repeat-blooming varieties of Climber. Strangely, if a variety is listed as being prone to mildew (as is Zéphirine Drouhin, for example) it may be more successful grown in a slightly shaded position, because hot walls encourage mildew. Bare north-facing aspects exposed to the worst of the elements are not conducive to growing even the hardiest of roses, however, and you should not attempt this. The ultimate test for such conditions would be Maigold, a prickly spreader, more a Shrub than a Climber; if this variety cannot be grown, then nothing else can.

▲ Altissimo is a Climber for all lovers of single roses. Here the color of its blooms picks up that of the window frame. This variety can also be grown as a freestanding shrub by shortening the main stems at pruning time.

Climbing roses on pergolas, arches, and pillars

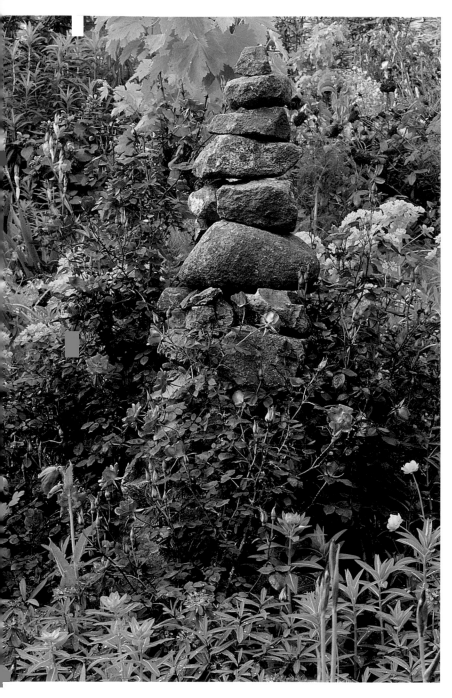

▲ *Warm Welcome is one of the best "patio climbers," the orange vermilion of its blooms beautifully set off by bronze-red foliage. Here it is trained to clothe and partially obscure this sculptural stone pyramid, a focal point of the garden.*

The traditional planting of roses on pergolas and arches calls for vigorous growers with a pliant habit which can be trained up the piers and across the top of the horizontal beams. The style of growth is the most important criterion when choosing a variety for this purpose; obviously a rigid upright grower would not be suitable. Fragrance is also a desirable asset in roses grown over arches and pergolas, under which people may walk and enjoy the sweet scent.

Ramblers were formerly chosen to clothe pergolas and arches, but they, of course, had a short mid-season flowering. The more recently introduced repeat-blooming Climbers are more appropriate, and, given careful training (see page 161), the larger, more vigorous varieties are suitable even in small gardens. Since they do not have the pliant growth of the Ramblers, they will require gentle manipulation of their more rigid growths before age hardens the wood. Twining the upright growths around the piers will, to a certain extent, encourage bloom, but generally the same principles apply as in training Climbers to grow horizontally in a fan shape. On a pergola, there is no reason why summer-flowering Ramblers such as Dorothy Perkins may not be used in conjunction with a less vigorous repeat-blooming rose, ensuring a colorful "roof" for the early part of the summer at least, while the vertical piers, clad in repeat-flowering varieties, can be colorful for longer. On a trellis pergola it makes sense to attach the shoots to the outside of the trellis, rather than letting them weave through the latticework, so that the rose can easily be taken down whenever necessary for the purposes of pruning, maintenance, and retraining.

Many rose catalogs refer to "pillar" roses; these are particular selections with a neat, upright-growing habit which are less likely to shoot upward, leaving a bare stem at the base of the plant. They are suitable for growing in restricted places that do not permit lateral growth, as well as for twining around to cover a freestanding pillar or obelisk. Growing Climbing roses on pillars, cones, or obelisks is

▲ *Climbing rose Handel is trained up the metal framework of this gazebo, enclosing a magnificent terracotta vase filled with sempervivums.*

another useful way of adding height to a rose bed or border. In some gardens, a line of posts may be connected by stringing heavy rope between their tops to form a continuous chain, along which Ramblers, with their lax growth, may be grown, turning the swathes of roses into an attractive feature when in flower.

Roses with large blooms may look out of proportion on small structures, and smaller-flowered varieties will sometimes be a more suitable choice. The recently introduced Climbing Miniature roses, otherwise known as "patio" climbers, such as King Tut, Warm Welcome, and Patio Queen, would provide the right scale for the small

garden, although some are too short for tall pillars and pyramids. Often produced on quite short stems of less than 3ft. (1m.) in height, they are also an asset in forming a grouping of containerized plants. These colorful small "trees" provide a useful structural element and, treated with care, will produce a wealth of bloom over a long season, as well as being easy to maintain. They are also useful on walls of restricted width, such as the space often found between windows, and may be excellent subjects to grow in containers where paving does not allow for planting directly into the soil. The containers should be at least 18in. (45cm.) in height and diameter, and provisions must be made for supporting and training their growth.

In general, the old-fashioned Ramblers, such as Albertine and Dorothy Perkins, are difficult to fit into the smaller garden, having only a short flowering season in the early summer, being prone to mildew when it is rife, and being difficult to prune properly to get the best results. Many of the more vigorous Climbing varieties are, in fact, quite large and therefore do not make good subjects for confined spaces. However, they do have their uses, and their pliable stems can be trained into mature trees of 20ft. (7m.) and more. Their vigorous stems will require some support to reach into the tree branches, as the rose should be planted at least 2ft. (60cm.) away from the base of the tree trunk. Varieties suitable for this purpose, and not mentioned elsewhere in this book, are: *Rosa filipes* var. 'Kiftsgate' (a monster which will grow to some 30ft. [10m.] and more), Rambling Rector, Alchymist, Wedding Day, Bobbie James, and François Juranville. Alchymist is rather shrubby, but the flowers are a charming yellow-shaded gold, while François Juranville has flowers of salmon-pink; the others are all white-flowered and possibly more spectacular.

In recent years Karl Hetzel, of Germany, has bred a number of repeat-blooming Ramblers under the names Super Fairy, Super Dorothy, Super Elfin, Super Excelsa, and Super Sparkler, which promise to be a great asset in the smaller garden. They are becoming very popular in Europe, where they are also budded onto stems to produce repeat-blooming weeping standards.

◄ *Hybrid Musk roses Buff Beauty and Felicia are both of a restrained height, making them suitable for a boundary hedge in this small country garden.*

Rose hedges

Rose hedges serve as an excellent structural feature in gardens large and small, providing colorful blooms for most of the summer. In rural surroundings, especially, there is immense scope for the use of a wide range of rose types, not necessarily of uniform height. Urban gardens may well call for a neater, more formal look, best achieved by selecting a compact-growing variety.

A hedge is only a line of plants doing a particular job; it could be merely 12in. (30cm.) tall, but might equally well be tree height. In a small garden we are, of course, considering the lower end of the scale, but much depends on the intended purpose. As knee-high hedges used to demarcate one part of the garden from another, without forming any part of a screen, the "patio" roses would be an excellent choice. One variety that would fit the bill superbly is Natchez, whose blooms smother the whole plant—one of the main criteria of a rose hedge. Many bedding roses bloom only on top of the bush, which would not be at all suitable. Choose a variety that flowers from the ground upward, avoiding bare stems at the base.

To achieve the most homogeneous effect, stick to a single variety, but so long as the outline of the planting as a whole is regular, there is no reason why you cannot mix varieties, especially if you wish to create an informal appearance. In order, however, to avoid the look of planting a job lot, it is a good idea to form a repeated pattern: ABABABAB, for example, or AABBAABBAABB, ABCABCABC, or even ABCBABCBAB. Using a mix of varieties gives ample scope for you to be creative and so long as the pattern of the mix is consistent, it will have a sense of continuity. Many Shrub or English roses make excellent taller hedges. I once saw a spectacular, but unlikely, hedge comprising a Rugosa hybrid alternating with *Rosa moyesii* 'Geranium', the difference between the thicket of the Rugosa and the twiggy, upright growth of the briar contrasing well, especially when both were loaded with brilliant orange hips in fall.

▲ *The yellow-flowered English rose Graham Thomas, underplanted by geraniums and Alchemilla mollis, makes a good divider in an informal small garden.*

Many people plant a prickly rose hedge as an intruder-proof boundary, which makes them feel secure and has the added bonus of blooms. Of reasonable proportions for a small garden, Rugosa hybrids, such as Frau Dagmar Hastrup, are very prickly, as are many of the Species roses. Rugosas, deeply planted, are good at regenerating shoots from the base which help to thicken the hedge at the bottom. Their hips and the golden color of their leaves in fall are additional features. Within the garden you may wish to screen off unsightly but necessary facilities, such as compost heaps, or toolsheds. Some of the taller Floribunda varieties, such as Iceberg and Mountbatten, make a good rose hedge for this purpose.

Growing roses in containers

In the small garden, roses may be grown in pots of all shapes and sizes to furnish a paved or gravelled area or to create effective "punctuation" in the open garden. Indeed, the use of tubs and urns on a patio, terrace, balcony, wooden deck, or rooftop is often the only way to grow roses in an urban area, and containers such as these have the added advantage of being mobile. Give some thought to their placement: containers may be positioned to suit a formal style, used either singly as a focal point or arranged in pairs —for example, two pot-grown standard roses might flank a doorway or steps—otherwise they can be grouped or massed together in a more informal way.

Any rose will grow in a container, provided the volume of soil or potting mixture is enough to sustain the size of plant. A "patio" rose, for instance, bought from the garden center in a container of 4 quarts (4 liters), or measuring 5in. (13cm.) across the top, needs to be replanted in at least double that volume of potting mix to enjoy a productive life. An average Climber or standard rose should be grown in a tub or pot with a diameter and depth of 20in. (50cm.). The foliage of Hybrid Teas and Floribundas is generally too coarse, and their habit of growth too heavy, for pots in a small garden.

The choice of containers and the material of which they are made, whether they be terracotta or ceramic, stone or wood, is a matter of personal preference. But the pot must have drainage holes drilled in the bottom, and its base should be well covered with crocks. If it is to stand on a flat surface, raise the container off the ground just enough to allow any excess water to drain away. Choose a growing medium suitable for woody plants, preferably a mixture based on the finest loam, adding well-rotted organic matter such as manure or garden compost and a source of potash (such as ashes from a fire). Plant roses into their pots between fall and early spring.

All the rules of good cultivation apply to roses grown in pots, since these plants depend totally on the attention you give them. Regular watering is essential, especially during dry weather; when you go on vacation, have somebody else water your containers. Roses need feeding during the growing season, so add a dash of liquid tomato food to the water at two-weekly intervals; its potash content will help ensure profuse blooming. Container-grown roses need light and air on all sides in order to develop evenly, so stand them slightly apart from other planting. Deadhead the blooms regularly, and prune in late winter/early spring (see page 152).

Container-grown roses will eventually become pot-bound, their soil mix shrunk and compacted by continual watering. Once every two or three years, take them out of their containers in spring, knock off any old soil mix clinging to the roots, and re-pot into fresh soil mix. In the intervening years pot-grown roses may be top-dressed, which involves removing a generous layer of old soil mix from the top of the container and replacing it with nutrient-rich new mix.

Choosing roses for containers

Used either on their own or in conjunction with other plants, container-grown roses will bring color and life to a small garden in summer. Grown alone, many of the newer types of rose are ideally suited to container culture, especially "patio" roses, "patio" climbers, and Ground Cover roses, with their small, neat foliage and fairly lax growth. The spreading habit of the more prostrate-growing varieties has also been used to great effect in hanging baskets. Plant in late autumn and leave the planted baskets outside until the roses become

▲ *An informal collection of potted plants in galvanized containers, including standard and patio roses, brings color and interest to this corner of a contemporary paved garden.*

◄ *Their colors, shapes, and fragrance make roses an ideal subject to grow in containers on a rooftop garden. The popular Floribunda, Iceberg, plays an important role in introducing long-lasting fragrance and color.*

established. After this, if you have an unheated glasshouse, they can be brought in and the early growths may be "assisted" to trail down over the edge of the basket. (If you do not have a greenhouse, leave them outside but bear in mind that they will not bloom until mid- to late summer.) Once all danger of frost is over, move the baskets outside. Water daily, adding a weekly feed of tomato food, with a high potash content, to feed both foliage and flowers.

In larger containers the planting need not be restricted to roses used singly; but, companions must be selected with care. In a group planting, choose from the multitude of rose shapes, sizes, and colors to contrast, or blend with, the enormous selection of well-textured foliage plants. Bear scale in mind at all times. It would be pointless to use the dainty, small-flowered varieties of "patio" or China roses with a large, glossy-leaved mahonia, for example. Choice of color is crucial to the impact of a display too. If the background is dark in tone, you may select a pale-colored rose to lift and brighten the area and so the blooms show up well against it.

Ideas for the best roses to grow successfully in containers and hanging baskets are suggested, right.

Variety	Code	Use	Colour
Aspen*	POULurt	PB	Lemon-yellow
Avon	POULmulti	PB	White
Crystal Palace*	POULrek	P	Creamy peach
Festival*	KORdialo	P	Crimson scarlet & white
Hertfordshire	KORtenay	PB	Carmine-pink
Kent*	POULcov	P	White
Lancashire*	KORstegli	PB	Crimson
Little White Pet		P	White
Mandarin*	KORcelin	P	Orange and pink
Natchez	POUlen	P	Palest pink
Pink Hit	POULtipe	P	Soft rose-pink
Queen Mother*	KORquemu	P	Soft pink
St. Boniface	KORmatt	P	Brilliant scarlet
Suffolk	KORmixal	PB	Crimson
The Fairy*		P	Soft pink
Top Marks	FRYministar	P	Vermilion-scarlet
Wiltshire*	KORmuse	PB	Bright rose-pink
White Flower Carpet*	NOASchnee	PB	White
Worcestershire	KORlalon	PB	Pale lemon

* = featured in this book   P = roses for pots   B = roses for baskets

Companions for roses

▲ *The delicate flowers of* Clematis 'Hybrida Sieboldii' *enhance the soft pink blooms of Climber New Dawn, one of the first repeat-blooming Climbing roses. Take care choosing varieties of clematis, which may need a pruning regime detrimental to that of roses. Different forms of the Jackmanii and Viticella families, which can be pruned almost to the ground in late winter or early spring, are the best to use.*

The multitude of colors and forms within the rose genus can be embellished in the garden by the introduction of contrasting or complementary plants from other families. Apart from contributing to a rich and varied border planting, companion plants are valuable for a number of reasons. They may be chosen to flower at a different season, to provide interest when the roses are not in bloom; or, simultaneous-flowering subjects may be selected specifically to enhance and offset the summer display of roses. Tall-growing shrubs will bring structure to a border, while low-growing subjects like spring bulbs and early summer perennials will shroud the bare stems of some roses, providing interest at ground level.

There are, it is true, some drawbacks to the practice of underplanting roses. Mulching is made more difficult, since it may smother low-growing plants, and there will be problems in applying much-needed food to your roses if the underplanting is too thick. Repeat blooming roses do not generally cope too well with very close competition from other plants, so it is important to allow your roses ample space, without spoiling the line and flow of a mixed border. However, all these disadvantages pale into insignificance against the beauty of a well-planted mixed border.

The bold and sculptural shape of many roses, their relatively large flower size, long flowering season, and wide range of colors gives them a vital role in the sucessful mixed border, where at least a third of the shrubs will be roses. In choosing companion plants for roses, bear in mind their height and flower shape as well as color, flowering time, foliage, texture, and perfume. While plants used at the front of a border need only be tall enough to hide any of the rose's bare stems, those at the back or center of the bed should have some structural value. The blooms of companion plants are usually smaller than those of the surrounding roses and may take an entirely different, contrasting form—such as the spikes of delphiniums and foxgloves or the feathery forms of gypsophila and *Crambe cordifolia*. Partnering roses with plants that have similar flower forms, like peonies and cistus, can—if there is a subtle color contrast and a difference in height—provide a shapely echo. However, using large-flowered peonies with roses in a bed, or clematis hybrids with dinner-plate sized blooms to partner Climbing roses on a wall, may not have the desired impact. In terms of underplanting, avoid invasive ground-covering plants such as ivies, bluebells, and Solomon's seal, which would deprive the roses of moisture and nutrients.

In early spring, bulbs bring color to a bed before roses even break into young growth. There is a range of crocuses, from white, through cream and shades of yellow, to mauves and deep purples, as well as delicate white snowdrops and blue muscari. The later spring bulbs—daffodils, narcissi, and tulips—can look wonderful peering through Ground Cover roses, and, by the time they are over, the roses will have started into growth, their leaves hiding the shriveling,

▲ Roses play a key part in this mixed border, with its variety of textures, colors, and shapes. The blooms of Little White Pet contrast effectively with the tall spires of foxgloves and the domes of clipped box, while pillar roses give height at the back of the bed.

▶ *In this vibrant color scheme, the yellow spires of verbascum and the lime-yellow leaves of golden hop offset the gray upright foliage of lychnis and the green leaves of the roses. The bright pink lychnis flowers and the rounded blooms of the scarlet Floribunda make a startling contrast.*

unsightly bulb foliage and allowing rejuvenating bulbs to mature naturally. Spring-flowering shrubs are useful partners too, providing interest even before, or at the same time as, the earliest Species roses. Early-flowering spiraeas, forsythia, and flowering currants (*Ribes*) may be somewhat hackneyed but provide effective splashes of color, followed by the gloriously fragrant lilacs in white, cream, pink, and purple.

Herbaceous perennials are classic summer-flowering subjects to plant amid Shrub roses in the mixed border. The tall spires of foxgloves, delphiniums, and hollyhocks give vertical relief to the rounded clumps of rose bushes. Among summer-flowering bulbs, lilies give an exotic touch, introducing a different range of hues. Late summer brings yet another flush of color to the garden in the form of asters, phlox, valerian, *Sedum spectabile* and *Anemone japonica*, followed by the crop of yellows, golds, oranges, and scarlets of autumn foliage and rose hips, haws, and brilliant berries.

When choosing partners, much depends on the type and habit of the roses in your mixed border. The vivid colors and hard lines of some Modern bedding roses, such as Hybrid Teas and Floribundas, can make them unsympathetic companions when used singly. They are better planted in small groups, in colors that complement their surroundings, with some mounded, bushy plants nearby to help disguise their rigid habit. Group planting in clumps avoids the confetti-like look of single planting and makes a greater impact. It also prevents single roses from getting lost in the abundant growth of other plants. Shrub roses, on the other hand, are often planted singly. A Shrub rose with rounded growth can become the focus in a border, while those with tall, arching growth, such as *Rosa moyesii* and *Rosa glauca*, or even Hybrid Tea roses Alexander and Congratulations, form an excellent contrast to lower plants. Old Shrub and English roses are best partnered by herbaceous perennials that contrast with or complement their rounded form and full, multi-petaled blooms. Roses look wonderful emerging from lower-growing plants like aquilegias or the light, feathery flowers of gypsophila or *Alchemilla mollis*, all of which set off the heavier, more "blobby" growth and flowers of Shrub roses.

Color combinations

One of the rose's great virtues is the wide range of color found within the genus and its many species and hybrids. In selecting companions, your aim is to find simultaneously flowering perennials, shrubs, and bulbs which pick up the color of the rose and enhance it, or to choose contrasting color plants to act as a foil. In mixed borders, a more subtle effect is produced if the color changes are achieved gradually, in drifts, rather than by jumping abruptly from one color to another.

Foliage color should also be taken into account in a mixed planting as it can become an important backdrop for roses. The silver leaves of *Stachys byzantina*, artemisias, and santolinas, and the glaucous leaves of lavender, senecio, and *Ruta graveolens* all provide an ideal foil for roses of all shades, whereas the golden-yellow shades found in many evergreen euonymus would completely kill the delicacy of a soft pink rose such as The Fairy or Cécile Brunner. On the other hand, either the golden-yellow of euonymus or the silvery gray of lavender and artemisia would form a tasteful combination with a cream or yellow rose, such as Aspen or Crystal Palace.

When thinking of color for contrast, one immediately turns to the various shades of blue, one of the hues missing from the spectrum of colors found among garden roses. The blue flower spikes of lavender in its many varieties blend beautifully with all shades of pink-flowered rose. Among the hardy perennials, the colors of *Geranium* 'Johnson's Blue' and *G.* 'Buxton's Blue,' of the hardy agapanthus, the various campanulas and catmint (*Nepeta* x *faassenii*) complement all shades of pink rose, except salmon pink. Purple foliage is also a good partner for pink roses: as found, for example, in low-growing *Ajuga reptans* 'Atropurpurea' and dark violas, as well as taller *Cotinus coggygria* and *Cosmos atrosanguineus*.

Whether we want to complement, blend with, or even tone down the impact of the brilliant vermilions and orange-reds of rose blooms, there are many plants to choose among the perennials, such as coreopsis, rudbeckia, daylilies and some of the shorter-growing sunflowers as well as heliopsis, another yellow daisy. Among the bedding annuals try such subjects as the marigolds as well as *Tagetes* (often grown among roses to attract hoverflies, deadly enemies of aphids). The deep reds and stronger

pinks generally look best next to purples and mauves. The yellow found in Modern roses can sometimes be difficult to accommodate; if it is harsh and garish, it will jar with most other flowers. But try yellow roses with bronze fennel and other plants with bronze-tinged foliage, as well as with blue-flowered plants such as *Salvia* x *superbum*, delphiniums, or blue penstemons. Pure yellows provide an effective contrast to rich blues, the paler shades verging on cream associating better with soft blues.

▲ *White lightens up a planting and adds a touch of elegance to a mixed border.* Geranium *'Kashmir White' shrouds the base of a full-petaled rose.*

▲ *The texture of flowing grasses emphasizes the glowing crimson blooms of patio rose Festival.*

A collection
of roses

Over the following pages will be found close-up photographic portraits of the best

roses for small gardens, showing their unique qualities and characteristics. They are

divided into Hybrid Teas, Floribundas, Climbing Roses, Ground Cover Roses, Shrub

Roses, and English Roses and individual descriptions can be found grouped together

at the end of each section. Under the name of the rose variety are other names it may

be known by, including, first, its international code name which comprises the name

of the breeder in its first three letters; where no code name is given, the rose predates

the practice of giving international names. Following each description is a summary of

the rose's vital statistics: its size (spread followed by height); the name of the breeder,

and the year it first appeared; parents' names where known; any major awards

received; and whether it has any fragrance. The abbreviations used for the awards are

explained in more detail on page 24.

Hybrid Teas

ROYAL WILLIAM

Still the best dark red rose, with
perfectly reflexed outer petals.

SELFRIDGES

A worldwide favorite for its fragrance and glorious color.

PEACE OF VEREENIGEN

An upright grower with dark foliage, which lasts well as a cut flower.

JUST JOEY

A strong, bushy grower with
large, frilly-edged blooms.

CONGRATULATIONS

An excellent rose for cutting,
with long, smooth stems.

VALENCIA

Large, sweetly scented buff-orange blooms, twice the size shown here.

PEACE

Surely one of the greatest roses of all time (shown here less than half its actual size).

DAWN CHORUS

Neat, fragrant blooms of a classic high-pointed shape (here enlarged to three times its size).

SILVER JUBILEE

One of the best roses of the twentieth
century, with beautiful scrolled blooms.

TEQUILA SUNRISE

A spectacular cocktail of a rose, appropriately named.

TYNWALD

An upright-growing rose whose rounded
buds open to large, many-petaled blooms.

Hybrid Teas

Previously known as Large-Flowered roses, this class of rose has now reverted to its original name, Hybrid Teas. The first popular varieties were introduced in the latter part of the nineteenth century, the early cultivars a result of crossing Hybrid Perpetuals with Tea roses, hence the name used in the early classification. It is extremely unlikely, however, that any modern Large-Flowered rose has a Tea rose in its parentage or even its ancestry. The stiff, upright-growing Hybrid Teas, with their scrolled buds and pointed blooms, differed greatly from the rosette-shaped roses of the past and were the start of a completely new approach to growing roses.

These bedding varieties of rose have classic-shaped flowers borne mainly at the top of the plant, either singly or in well-spaced clusters of two or three blooms. The blooms can vary from the slim, neat, high-centered shape offered by florists as a cut flower, to large, full, multi-petaled blooms. The plants themselves may be either upright, elegant specimens up to 2ft. (60cm.) tall; bushy, many-branched shrubby growers; or tall, stately bushes up to 6ft. (2m.) in height.

The early colors of red, pink, and white were enhanced by the addition of yellow and orange in the early 1900s, and the luminous cinnabar-reds in the 1950s, which in turn gave rise to the brilliant vermilion-scarlets of today. By careful yet rigorous selection, varieties have been chosen to produce blooms in quantity, possessing characteristics that make ideal florist's cut flowers. The qualities looked for in a florist's cut flower are somewhat different from those traditionally required in a garden flower. These include an elegant, high-pointed, scrolled shape, the trait of showing the true color from the moment the bud opens, and petals that remain crisp and unfading for a long time, even when the flowers crumple and die.

CONGRATULATIONS *Page 58*

Synonyms: KORlift; Sylvia

A tall-growing rose, sometimes classified as a Floribunda, though it tends to grow one on a stem, rather than in clusters. Its height makes it eminently suited to planting toward the back of a border. The clear rose-pink blooms of elegant classic shape are borne on long, smooth, almost thornless stems. They last for almost a week when cut, which makes Congratulations a deserved favorite among flower arrangers. A paler pink sport of this variety was chosen by the U.K. National Association of Flower Arrangers Societies (NAFAS) to celebrate its thirtieth anniversary, under the appropriate name 'Pink Pearl.' The matte foliage is pale green, shaded maroon when young.

Size *2 x 4ft. (60 x 120cm.)*
Raiser *Kordes, Germany 1979*
Parentage *Carina x seedling*
Slight fragrance

DAWN CHORUS *Page 60*

Synonym: DICquasar

The neat, crisply petaled, scented blooms of Dawn Chorus are borne in quite large, well-spaced clusters on a medium height bush of compact bushy habit. The classic high-pointed flowers are very long lasting and have become popular among flower arrangers, who do not mind the short stems. Coppery red foliage makes an admirable foil for the

tangerine and bright orange-yellow blooms of exquisite shape. A popular bedding rose selected by the British rose growing industry as their Rose of the Year in 1993.

Size *2 x 2ft. (60 x 60cm.)*
Raiser *Dickson, U.K. 1993*
Parentage *Wishing x Peer Gynt*
Awards *Gold Medal, Dublin 1993; Certificate of Merit, Glasgow 1995*
Fragrant

INGRID BERGMAN *Page 56*

Synonym: POULman

The large, glowing dark red blooms of Ingrid Bergman represent a fine tribute to one of the classic beauties of the film industry. The scrolled-shape flowers are borne erect on sturdy stems, making this rose excellent for cutting and for exhibiting. But its real virtue lies in the extreme weather resistance of the crisp petals, which makes it an asset for any rose bed or mixed border. It is well furnished with glossy, dark green foliage. The blooms also have a slight scent, though not the deep, luscious fragrance one expects from a red rose.

Size *2 x 3ft. (60 x 90cm.)*
Raiser *Poulsen, Denmark 1986*
Awards *TGC, RNRS; Gold Medal Belfast*
Slight fragrance

JUST JOEY *Page 57*

Coppery orange-red, high-pointed buds open to exciting frilly-edged, extra large

apricot-buff blooms which, as they open, develop pink shading at the edge of the petals. The open, rather loosely angular plant is well clothed in matte bronze-red leaves, maturing to deepest bronze-green.

This well known and highly popular variety was named by its raiser after his wife. It was voted "World's Favorite Rose" by a congress of the World Federation of Rose Societies in New Zealand in 1994.

Size *2 x 2ft. (60 x 60cm.)*
Raiser *R. Pawsey (Cants of Colchester), U.K. 1973*
Awards *TGC, RNRS; JMMM*
Fragrant

PEACE *Page 59*

Synonyms: Gloria Dei, Madame A. Meilland, Gioia

One of the most famous roses of all time and possibly the best loved, although some would disagree.

Peace is a large grower, whose strong constitution makes it a taller plant than many gardeners anticipate, especially when it is not pruned. Raised in the late 1930s, Peace was not introduced until after the end of World War II, when it was presented at the inaugural assembly of the United Nations, hence the name.

The slightly fragrant blooms can be among the largest in the rose garden, somewhat changeable in color with different soil conditions and climates. It has in fact produced several mutations of color during its long life.

The large, rounded buds are usually deep yellow with splashes of red, opening to large, frilly, pale yellow blooms lightly edged pink. The heavy, leathery foliage is deep glossy green.

Size *4 x 4ft. (120 x 120cm.)*
Raiser *Meilland, France 1939*
Awards *Gold Medal RNRS; Gold Medal Portland, Oregon 1944; AARS 1946; Gold Medal ARS 1947; Award of Garden Merit, RHS; many others*
Light fragrance

PEACE OF VEREENIGEN

Page 55

Synonyms: KORverpea; Cleopatra, Kleopatra, New Kleopatra

Not to be confused with an earlier (1950s) variety of the same name (Cleopatra), the same color and—to make matters even more confusing—from the same raiser. This variety is an upright grower with fine, high-centered blooms of medium size, sometimes borne in clusters, though more often not. The blooms are glowing crimson-scarlet within and deep harvest-gold on the reverse of the petals. The deep bronze-green foliage is tinted reddish bronze when young and, together with the dark purplish stems, makes a perfect foil for the blooms. A good variety for cutting.

Size *20in. x 2½ft. (50 x 75cm.)*
Raiser *Kordes, Germany 1994*
Award *TGC, RNRS*
Slight fragrance

ROYAL WILLIAM *Page 53*

Synonyms: KORzaun; Duftzauber "84," Fragrant Charm, Leonore Christian

The deep crimson blooms have the classical shape with perfectly reflexed outer petals. The fragrance is the luscious fruity perfume one expects from the crimson roses, yet the petals are crisp and unfading. What makes this such an outstanding rose is the robust and healthy growth with disease-resistant foliage, deep maroon-red when young, aging to dark bronze-green.

Selected by the British rose growing industry as their Rose of the Year in 1987, it was also awarded the James Mason Memorial Medal for having given special pleasure to rose-loving gardeners in 1999.

Size *2 x 3ft. (60 x 90cm.)*
Raiser *Kordes, Germany 1984*
Parentage *Feuerzauber x seedling*
Awards *Award of Garden Merit, RHS; TGC, RNRS; JMMM 1999*
Very fragrant

SELFRIDGES *Page 54*

Synonyms: KORpriwa; Berolina

Bright yellow with amber-yellow shading, the blooms are of good shape and size. The sweet "Tea" fragrance has made this a yellow rose to cherish, though its extreme vigor will often produce canes of almost 6ft. (2m.) in height, so it will require careful placing at the back of the border. The semi-glossy foliage is bright green, and it is a fine rose for cutting

because of the long, smooth stems and very few thorns.

The name 'Selfridges' came from the London department store of that name to celebrate the centennial of the birth of Gordon Selfridge, its American founder.

Size *2 x 4ft. (60 x 120cm.) and more*
Raiser *Kordes, Germany 1984*
Fragrant

SILVER JUBILEE *Page 61*

A superb variety with spectacular blooms borne in great profusion. Although it is best suited for bedding, providing a mass of color, the blooms when disbudded become quite large and will win prizes on the show bench.

The color may be described as apricot-salmon shades with a deeper reverse, while rose pink is often to be seen within the petals. The distinctive medium-green foliage is large and luxuriant. The plant, upright yet bushy, is a handsome specimen, though well-endowed with thorns.

Named to commemorate the Silver Jubilee of H.M. Queen Elizabeth II, this rose is also a fitting memorial to its raiser, the late Alec Cocker of Aberdeen.

Size *2 x 2½ft. (60 x 75cm.)*
Raiser *Cocker, U.K. 1978*
Parentage *[(Highlight x Colour Wonder) x (Parkdirektor Riggers x Piccadilly)] x Mischief*
Awards *PIT, RNRS 1977; Gold Medal Portland, Oregon 1981; JMMM 1985*
Some fragrance

TEQUILA SUNRISE *Page 62*

Synonyms: DICobar; Beaulieu

A spectacular cocktail of a rose. Its petals, dark and bunched-up when in tight bud, explode to reveal a deep golden yellow bloom, heavily edged and shaded brilliant scarlet, developing into a tangerine-orange shade as the bloom matures. The glossy bronze-green foliage is lightly tinted maroon in its juvenile stage and smothers the compact-growing plant. The blooms are sometimes borne in shapely clusters and other times singly. A fascinating variety to cut and watch closely as it opens.

Size *2 x 2ft. (60 x 60cm.)*
Raiser *Dickson, N. Ireland 1989*
Awards *Gold Medal, RNRS 1988; Gold Medal Belfast*
Slight fragrance

TYNWALD *Page 63*

Synonym: MATwyt

A tall, upright rose with distinctive rounded buds of ivory white, lightly tinted pale lemon yellow, often borne in clusters but mostly singly. They open to large, rounded, many-petaled blooms initially giving the impression of a white rose but on closer examination proving to be delicately shaded lemon yellow and soft pink in the inner folds of the petals.

Often growing quite tall, this rose is suited to a position at the back of a border, and it can, if pruned with care, grow into a tall, handsome shrub.

It was named in 1979 to commemorate the millennium of Tynwald, the Manx (Isle of Man, U.K.) parliament, the oldest continuous legislature in the world.

Size *2 x 4ft. (60 x 120cm.)*
Raiser *Mattock, U.K. 1979*
Parentage *Peer Gynt x Isis*
Fragrant

VALENCIA *Page 59*

Synonyms: KOReklia; New Valencia, Valeccia

Very large blooms of buff-orange with golden shading are often of such exquisite form that Valencia receives top prizes in flower shows. The fine sweet and fruity fragrance endures, attracting people to bury their nose in the multitude of petals. A good rose for cutting, it flowers continuously throughout the summer and fall. It can suffer damage in wet weather, when its blooms may "ball up."

A vigorous grower which could be placed in the middle of a rose bed.

Size *2 x 3ft. (60 x 90cm.)*
Raiser *Kordes, Germany 1989*
Awards *HE Medal for fragrance 1989; Gold Medal, RNRS*
Very fragrant

Floribundas

SHOCKING BLUE

An incredible fragrance in an unusual color.

LIVIN' EASY

The fragrant, hot-colored
blooms are a real eye-catcher.

SUNSET BOULEVARD

Especially good seen against a dark
evergreen background.

LAVAGLUT

One of the darkest red roses; its semi-double blooms are borne in large clusters.

TRUMPETER

A low bushy grower whose blooms are
as jazzy as its namesake (shown here
twice its actual size).

ANNA LIVIA

A fine bedding rose which is deservedly popular for its even growth and showy blooms (in reality two-thirds of the size shown here).

FREDENSBORG

Named (British) Rose of the Year in 1999, this beautiful compact-growing variety is ideal for a small garden. It is shown here at half its true size.

MARIANDEL

A fine bedding rose with a well-deserved
reputation for good health.

SWEET DREAM
An attractive soft-colored
variety for a limited space.

ORANGES AND LEMONS

A scented rose with an exotic difference.

QUEEN MOTHER

An elegant rose named to celebrate
Her Majesty's ninetieth birthday.

FESTIVAL

A neat, rounded grower with luxuriant foliage.

CRYSTAL PALACE

A low-growing cluster-flowered rose with larger blooms than most patio roses (actually twice the size shown).

SUNSPRITE

Remarkable for its sweet
perfume, unusual in a
yellow variety.

MANDARIN

A whorl of petals showing a remarkable blend
of colors (shown four times its real size here).

ICEBERG

Still one of the best white
roses ever produced (two-
thirds the size shown).

HANNAH GORDON

Perfectly formed blooms in well-shaped clusters,
here shown at four times its actual size.

Floribundas

Formerly named Cluster-flowered roses, Floribunda bedding roses bear their flowers in trusses or clusters, with many blooms opening at the same time. The great trusses of bloom that are characteristic of the Floribundas are influenced by the Polyantha Pom-poms (now rarely grown because of their susceptibility to mildew), with a petal texture inherited from their Hybrid Tea forebears. Even farther back in their ancestry, the China rose had a strong influence. Floribunda flowers provide massed drifts of color through the garden, rather than producing individual specimens of perfect shape for close scrutiny. In truth, however, the inflorescences of many Floribunda varieties are quite as beautiful as their larger-flowered relatives.

The size and shape of bloom can vary enormously, from the dainty five-petaled varieties reminiscent of their wild rose ancestors, to the shapely, many-petaled specimens so close to the large-flowered Hybrid Tea roses. The height does not form any part of the definition of a Floribunda. These plants may range from the dwarf

cultivars, now classified separately as patio roses, to giants which may reach 6ft. (2m.) high, or even taller if left unpruned, such as 'The Queen Elizabeth' rose. Some Floribundas, though not many, have inherited a fragrance that is quite as good as anything else to be found in the rose world.

The patio roses, selected from dwarf (up to 20in. [50cm.]) compact-growing Floribunda roses and larger-growing Miniature roses, are popular in modern gardens. They are ideal to grow in containers to enhance paved areas where direct planting would be impossible, or where the only room available is in small beds in which the larger Hybrid Teas and Floribundas would be out of place. Patio roses are also excellent subjects for planting at the front of shrub borders, as well as for edging paths. Many fine patio varieties are also sold as potted plants which, given care and attention, will add color to sunroom plantings and for short periods of time may be grown as houseplants.

ANNA LIVIA *Page 74*

Synonyms: KORmetter; Sandton Beauty, Trier 2000

The large double rose pink blooms have the merest hint of salmon, although it takes a keen eye to detect it. The clusters of bloom are particularly well shaped, often with ten or more flowers in the truss at one time. This showy variety is quite awe-inspiring when planted en masse. The bushy plant produces very even growth, which makes Anna Livia one of the best bedding varieties. It has a light, refreshing fragrance.

The name 'Anna Livia' is taken from James Joyce's book *Finnegan's Wake* and commemorates the millennium of Dublin, the Irish capital, in 1998.

Size *2 x 2½ft. (60 x 75cm.)*

Raiser *Kordes, Germany 1985*

Parentage *(seedling x Tornado) x seedling*

Awards *Award of Garden Merit, RHS; Gold Medal Glasgow 1991; Gold Medal Orléans 1987*

Light fragrance

CRYSTAL PALACE *Page 81*

Synonyms: POULrek; Cristel Palace

Patio rose. A low-growing cluster-flowered variety somewhat different from the other patio roses in that the blooms are larger and the bush less compact. The delightful blooms have been described as "light peachy cream" in color and its delicate shading gives the variety its great and unique charm.

Size *2 x 2ft. (60 x 60cm.)*

Raiser *Poulsen Denmark 1995*

Slight fragrance

FESTIVAL *Page 81*

Synonym: KORdialo

Patio rose. An attractive variety bearing large clusters of blooms 2–3in. (6–7cm.) across. They are bright crimson-scarlet with a silvery white reverse to the petals, giving a bicolored appearance to the opening buds. The crimson flower then opens with a silvery white zone at the heart, accenting the golden boss of stamens.

This low-growing, rounded bush makes an ideal subject for planting at the edge of a flower bed or in a planter. The foliage is dark holly green with an attractive gloss.

Size *18 x 18in. (45 x 45cm.)*

Raiser *Kordes, Germany 1993*

Parentage *Regensberg x seedling*

Awards *TGC, RNRS; Rose of the Year 1994*

Slight fragrance

FREDENSBORG *Page 76*

Synonym: POULmax, Fascination

Dark green glossy foliage clothes this bedding rose, which bears attractive clusters of fragrant coral-pink blooms. This neat, compact grower makes a superb subject for the smaller garden, whether grown in beds or borders of limited size, or in planters such as large urns or pots.

After two years of exhaustive testing by the British rose industry, this variety was chosen as their "Rose of the Year" in 1999.

Size *2 x 2ft. (60 x 60cm.)*

Raiser *Poulsen, Denmark 1999*

Award *RNRS*

Fragrant

HANNAH GORDON *Page 85*

Synonyms: KORweiso; Raspberry Ice

A delightful confection of shades of pink, varying from palest blush, almost white, within the flower, to deep cherry pink on the edges of the petals. The shades vary, depending on the intensity of sunlight, and deepen as the bloom ages. The flowers are borne in well-spaced, moderately sized clusters on an upright-growing bush.

The shape of the flower buds, their exotic coloring, and the sparsely thorned stems make this cluster-flowered rose popular for use as a cut flower. It is an excellent variety for all gardens.

Size *2 x 2½ft. (60 x 75cm.)*

Raiser *Kordes, Germany 1983*

Parentage *seedling x Bordure (Strawberry Ice)*

Awards *TGC, RNRS 1983*

Slight fragrance

ICEBERG *Page 84*

Synonyms: KORbin; Fée des Neige, Schneewittchen

Introduced in 1958, Iceberg is still one of the most widely planted roses. This bushy, almost shrubby grower has semi-double, well-formed pure white flowers. Sometimes the white flowers display a slight blush, especially in cooler weather; and, as with all white roses, any damage is immediately visible; for example, raindrops that do not dry off right away may leave pink spots. The flowers, which are borne in clusters of up to a dozen at one time, have a delicate wild-rose perfume.

Iceberg can be used for many purposes: as a bedding rose, as a Shrub rose, as a hedge; and as a standard (Tree) rose among the best. It has even produced a climbing sport which is most useful, spreading as it does to some 12–15ft. (4–5m.) and flowering at the height of summer.

Size *2½ x 3½ft. (75 x 110cm.)*
Raiser *Kordes, Germany 1958*
Parentage *Robin Hood x Virgo*
Awards *Gold Medal RNRS 1958; Gold Medal, Baden Baden 1983; World's Favorite Rose 1983; Award of Garden Merit, RHS*
Slight fragrance

LAVAGLUT *Page 72*

Synonyms: KORlech; Intrigue; Lavaglow

One of the deepest red roses currently offered in rose catalogs. The large clusters of blackish crimson blooms often have up to 24 flowers. These semi-double blooms are particularly beautiful when seen in strong sunlight and retain their color until they drop.

A strong, bushy grower of medium height, well clothed in dark bronze-green foliage, it is an excellent rose for all gardens due to its almost nonstop performance during the flowering season, from midsummer until the first frosts of autumn.

Size *2 x 2ft. (60 x 60cm.)*
Raiser *Kordes, Germany 1981*
Parentage *Gruss an Bayern x seedling*
Awards *TGC, RNRS 1980*
Slight fragrance

LIVIN' EASY *Page 70*

Synonyms: HARwelcome; Fellowship

One of the brightest colored Floribunda roses; the glowing orange-vermilion flowers are freely produced in shapely clusters. The well-formed Hybrid Tea-shaped buds open to cupped blooms with attractive rounded petals, revealing golden stamens.

This vigorous bushy plant, well clothed with dark shiny foliage, is reputedly very disease resistant. For those who admire "hot" colors, it is an excellent choice to enliven a dull (but not shady) spot in the garden, though is not for the fainthearted!

Size *2 x 2½ft. (60 x 75cm.)*
Raiser *Harkness, U.K. 1992*
Parentage *Southampton x Remember Me*
Awards *Gold Medal RNRS; AARS 1996; Gold Medal, Portland, Oregon, 1998*
Slight fragrance

MANDARIN *Page 83*

Synonym: KORcelin

Patio rose. Shades of gold, orange, pink, and even red are shot through the small rosette-shaped flowers of this neat little bush. As the blooms open fully, the pink is accentuated, the orange grows paler, and the rosette becomes denser while the petals take on a slightly fluted appearance. The dark stems are stiffly upright and are furnished with attractive dark green foliage, which makes this a superb subject for a small rose bed set in a terrace or other paved area.

Size *18 x 18in. (45 x 45cm.)*
Raiser *Kordes, Germany 1987*
Awards *Gold Medal, Glasgow 1994; Certificate of Merit, Dublin*
Slight fragrance

MARIANDEL *Page 77*

Synonyms: KORpeahn; Carl Philip Kristian IV, The Times

Winner of many international awards, this fine rose was named 'The Times' in the United Kingdom to celebrate the two-hundredth anniversary of the founding of the great London newspaper.

The rosette flowers, borne in well-shaped clusters, are of glowing crimson-scarlet with deeper shades within the unfolding petals. Both blooms and foliage have good weather resistance. The juvenile foliage is tinged red and matures into darkest green, which retains a purplish, almost black hue. This

excellent bedding variety can also be used to make a low-growing hedge.
Size *2 x 2½ft. (60 x 75cm.)*
Raiser *Kordes, Germany 1986*
Parentage *Tornado x Redgold*
Awards *PIT, RNRS 1982; Golden Rose of the Hague 1990; Certificate of Merit, Belfast*
Slight fragrance

ORANGES AND LEMONS
Page 79

Synonyms: MACanlorem; Papagena

A rose for those looking for something exotic, perhaps for a hot-colored bed. Large, full blooms of golden yellow with stripes and flecks of deep tangerine orange are carried in small clusters on a taller-than-average bush. The long stems make this a suitable Floribunda for cutting, introducing something special for the flower arranger.

The deep bronze-green, glossy foliage is tinted reddish purple when young. The taller shoots, when trained, can turn 'Oranges and Lemons' into a shrub or even a short pillar rose.
Size *2 x 3½ft. (60 x 110cm.)*
Raiser *McGredy, New Zealand 1993*
Parentage *Roller Coaster x New Year (Arcadian)*
Award *TGC, RNRS 1991*
Slight fragrance

QUEEN MOTHER *Page 80*

Synonyms: KORquemu; Queen Mum

Patio rose. A delightfully elegant rose

chosen to celebrate Her Majesty's ninetieth birthday, this variety naturally became a popular choice when the Queen Mother achieved her century in the year 2000.

The simple, semi-double, soft pink blooms have great charm, showing up well against the glossy, dark green foliage. This vigorous shrubby plant of low to medium height is a fine variety, showing a distinct relationship to a host of recently bred Kordes varieties, with their characteristic resistance to disease.
Size *2 x 2ft. (60 x 60cm.)*
Raiser *Kordes, Germany 1991*
Awards *Award of Garden Merit, RHS*
Delicate fragrance

SHOCKING BLUE *Page 69*
Synonym: KORblue

One of the best of the so-called "blue" roses. Shocking Blue was first introduced in Germany as a cut flower variety, but having been tested in the garden, it soon found favor among gardeners looking for something out of the ordinary. The magenta buds are shaded and splashed deep plum purple, and the opening petals reveal a rich lilac-magenta flower with a very heavy scent.

To get the full benefit of the unusual shade, it is a good idea to plant it alongside a lemon yellow flower or golden-foliaged plant; otherwise the color does not stand out sufficiently against its deep bronze-green foliage. As

with many varieties, it requires deadheading to ensure continuity of bloom.
Size *2 x 3½ft. (60 x 110cm.)*
Raiser *Kordes, Germany 1985*
Parentage *Silver Star x seedling*
Very fragrant

SUNSET BOULEVARD
Page 71

Synonym: HARbabble

Named to celebrate and publicize the musical of the same name, 'Sunset Boulevard' was selected by the British rose industry as their Rose of the Year in 1997.

Well-shaped elegant buds of glowing orange-salmon open to reveal an intriguing shade of orange-apricot amid crisp unfolding petals. The slightly fragrant blooms are borne continuously on an upright but compact-growing plant, well-furnished with medium green semi-matte foliage. This variety is seen at its best against a dark green background.
Size *2 x 2½ft. (60 x 75cm.)*
Raiser *Harkness, U.K. 1997*
Parentage *Harold MacMillan x Fellowship*
Awards *TGC, RNRS 1996; Rose of the Year 1997*
Slight fragrance

SUNSPRITE *Page 82*

Synonyms: KORresia; Friesia; Korresia

Still one of the best yellow bedding roses. The large Hybrid Tea-shaped blooms are borne, sometimes singly and sometimes in clusters, in close succession and are of brilliant clear yellow which – rare for a rose in this color – does not fade. Another unusual feature of Sunsprite is that it has a strong fragrance, which has won it awards.

A vigorous, bushy plant of average height, it is well furnished with an abundance of glossy, bright green foliage and makes an excellent hedge. The blooms shatter on maturity, making deadheading unnecessary.

Size *2 x 2½ft. (60 x 75cm.)*
Raiser *Kordes, Germany 1977*
Parentage *Friedrich Worlein x Spanish Sun*
Awards *James Alexander Gamble Award for fragrance 1979; JMMM 1989; Gold Medal, Baden Baden*
Very fragrant

SWEET DREAM *Page 78*

Synonyms: FRYminicot; Sweet Dreams

Patio rose. Clusters of creamy apricot round buds open to reveal rosette-shaped, peachy apricot-colored blooms with deeper shades within the unfurling petals. The clusters may vary from just two or three to a whole wide-spreading head of many blooms borne on a strong upright stem. The plants often send up quite tall shoots, and some have even been trained as mini-climbers, but if you want a small, cushion-like plant, trim off these tall shoots low to achieve the desired effect. Whichever way it is

treated, Sweet Dream is a good rose for low edging, for mixed plantings, and for use in containers.

Size *2 x 2ft. (60 x 60cm.)*
Raiser *Fryer, U.K. 1988*
Parentage *seedling x [(Anytime x Liverpool Echo) x (New Penny x seedling)]*
Awards *JMMM 1998; Award of Garden Merit, RHS; Rose of the Year 1988*
Slight fragrance

TRUMPETER *Page 73*

Synonym: MACtru

The name of this rose celebrates the great jazz trumpeter Louis Armstrong after whom the parent plant (Satchmo) was also named.

The brilliant glowing scarlet blooms are carried in large, heavy trusses, on a bushy, almost spreading plant of low to medium growth. This fine bedding variety requires planting toward the front of a mixed bed, where its color would contrast beautifully with some of the blue-flowered herbaceous perennials.

Blooming from early summer till the first autumnal frost, Trumpeter is of tremendous value in the garden.

Size *2 x 2ft. (60 x 60cm.)*
Raiser *McGredy, New Zealand 1977*
Parentage *Satchmo x seedling*
Awards *Star of the South Pacific, New Zealand 1977; TGC, RNRS; JMMM 1991; Award of Garden Merit, RHS*
Slight fragrance

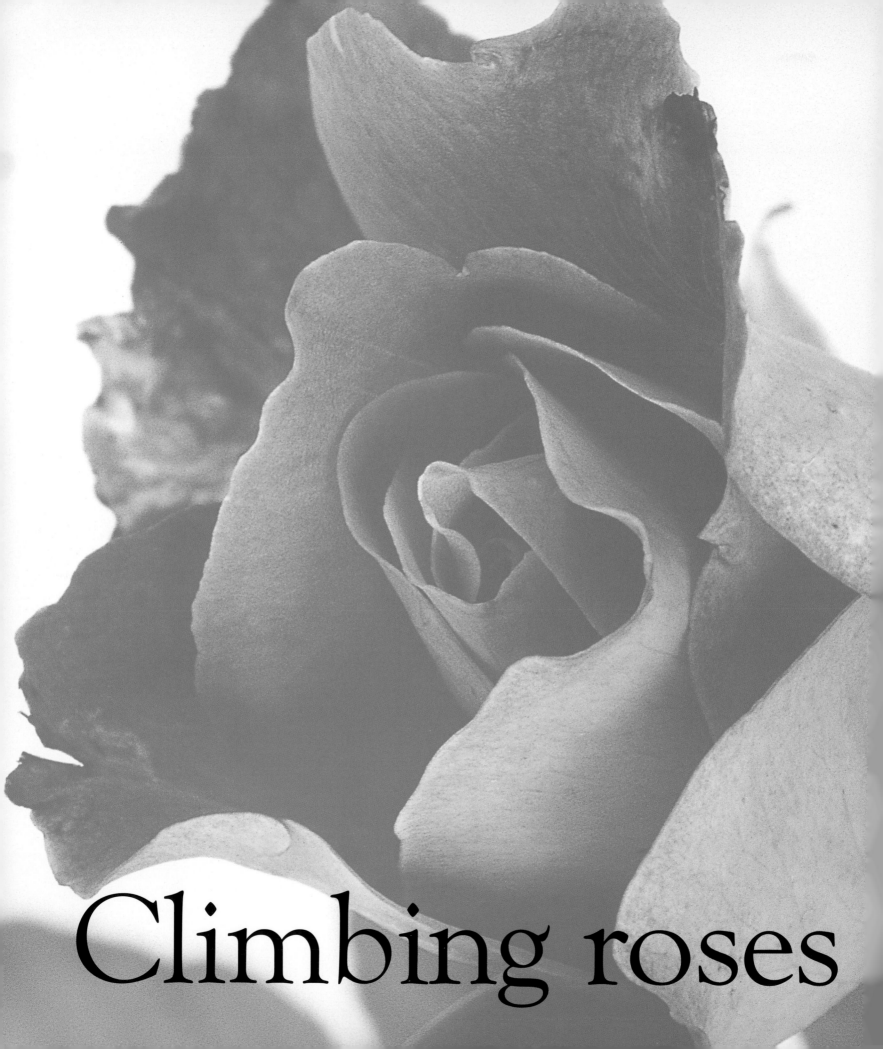

Climbing roses

FREISINGER MORGENROTE

Can be grown as a restrained
climber or a wide-arching shrub.

WARM WELCOME

Blooms of unusual brilliance (shown here one and a half times
their actual size) show up well against the bronze-red foliage.

PATIO QUEEN

The sweetly fragrant blooms are perfectly shaped.

COMPASSION

One of the best Modern Climbing
roses, vigorous and sweetly scented.

MADAME ALFRED CARRIÈRE

Now into its second century and still one of
the most popular varieties of Climber.

SWAN LAKE

Particularly beautiful on late autumnal evenings.

DREAMING SPIRES

The large, golden-yellow, semi-double blooms are very fragrant.

JOSEPH'S COAT

Can be grown equally well as
a Climber or a Shrub rose.

SUMMER WINE

A vigorous grower whose blooms are of
a glorious color and sweetly scented.

KING TUT

The neatness of the bloom is echoed in the formation of the cluster.

MERMAID

A famous Old rose with single blooms, combining great vigor and elegance.

ALTISSIMO

Single, saucer-shaped blooms appeal to all lovers of single roses.

TRADITION

A vigorous Climber to replace the old red Ramblers
on walls, fences, trellises, pergolas, and tall pillars.

SPECTACULAR

A popular Climber dating from the middle of the last century, it will tolerate being planted in semi-shade.

RAMIRA

Can be treated as a Climber or a loose-growing
Shrub, with large, cup-shaped soft pink blooms.

PENNY LANE

An elegant new Climber likely to
be with us for many years to come.

GRAND HOTEL

Blooms throughout summer and fall with
double crimson flowers and bronze-red foliage.

BABY RAMBLER

Large clusters of bloom (over twice the size shown here) smother the shrublike growth of this choice variety.

HANDEL

A neat *boutonnière* of a rose in white and deep pink.

Climbing roses

In the early part of the twentieth century most Climbing roses were the result of mutations from bush or bedding forms of rose. They were described under such names as Climbing Crimson Glory, i.e. a climbing form of the bush rose Crimson Glory. In addition, up until a few years ago most climbers bloomed for a matter of a few weeks only, from early to midsummer. The lax-growing Ramblers, an inheritance from the late eighteenth century, bloomed madly for even less time—two to three weeks —and then became a mass of new growth to provide bloom in the following summer. A few Ramblers that still exist may find a place in the smaller garden, to climb up into a tree or to camouflage a shed.

There were, in addition, some climbing varieties that were repeat blooming climbers from their seedling stages. A few of them survive, including one or two varieties illustrated in the following pages. Today's catalogs and garden centers still offer a few of the once-only flowering varieties, but on the whole, the Climbing roses currently being introduced belong to the repeat-blooming category. Flowering, as they do, on the current year's growth, they require almost no pruning to produce their magnificent crops of bloom.

The recently developed patio climbers, or climbing Miniatures, are tailor-made for the smaller garden, where space can easily be found for them. Raised in the U.K. in the 1980s and 1990s by Chris Warner, they represent one of the major breakthroughs in modern rose breeding. The blooms, in scale with the size of the plant and its foliage, are borne in clusters, and, most valuable of all, they flower from top to toe: it is rare to find a patio climber without bloom from early summer until (in temperate zones) fall. Used to fill the small spaces on walls of restricted size, they grow to 3ft. (1m.) across and up to 8ft. (2.5m.) tall.

Patio climbers may also be planted in large urns or tubs, on pillars and pergolas, as well as being grown in small beds as self-supporting shrubs.

ALTISSIMO *Page 100*

Synonyms: DELmur; Altus; Sublimely Single

A rose for the aficionado of single blooms. The dark crimson Hybrid Tea-shaped buds open to rich crimson-scarlet saucer-shaped blooms, revealing rich golden stamens. The stiff, upright branches can reach 12ft. (4m.) in height, but are best trained into a fan shape to ensure that the blooms are produced all along the horizontal branches.

Altissimo can also be grown as a vigorous upright shrub by shortening the main stems to form the height and outline desired. This will then produce many lateral shoots, carrying in wide clusters its blooms of great beauty.

Size *10–12ft. (3–4m.)*
Raiser *Delbard-Chabert, France 1966*
Parentage *Tenor x seedling*
Award *Award of Garden Merit, RHS*
Slight fragrance

BABY RAMBLER *Page 104*

Synonyms: CHEWramb; Little Rambler

Patio climber. Tiny globular buds of palest rose pink open to reveal rosette-shaped flowers, packed with petals. Very large clusters of bloom smother this shrubby grower, whose pliant main stems can grow to 6ft. (2m.) on a mature plant.

The plentiful, disease-resistant glossy dark green foliage is in perfect scale with the size of the bloom, with the superb fragrance making this a choice variety for the smaller garden.

Size *6ft. (2m.)*
Raiser *Warner, U.K. 1995*
Parentage *(Cécile Brunner x Baby Faurax) x (Marjorie Fair x Nozomi)*
Award *Certificate of Merit, RNRS*
Very fragrant

COMPASSION *Page 94*

Synonym: Belle de Londres

One of the greatest of modern Climbers, and the recipient of many awards. Large Hybid Tea-shaped, sweetly scented blooms of soft salmon pink, often with apricot-buff shadings, are borne singly or in clusters.

The perfect choice for the small garden with room for only one Climbing rose, whether it be fan-shaped on a wall or fence, grown up a pillar or obelisk, or trained on a pergola. It blooms for a long season; flowers have even been gathered on Christmas Day.

Size *8–10ft. (2.5–3m.)*
Raiser *Harkness, U.K. 1973*
Parentage *White Cockade x Prima Ballerina*
Awards *HE Medal for fragrance 1973; Gold Medal, Baden-Baden 1975; Gold Medal, Geneva 1975; Award of Garden Merit, RHS*
Very fragrant

DREAMING SPIRES *Page 96*

Deep golden buds open to large, semi-double, very fragrant, golden yellow blooms which fade to palest apricot as they age. Heavy dark green foliage clothes the tall, upright grower which repays being trained into a fan shape by producing a fine crop of blooms all summer and fall along each branch.

Raised by Robert H. Mattock from a cross between a leggy Bush rose and a vigorous Floribunda. It is named for Oxford, called the "City of dreaming spires" by poet Matthew Arnold in "*The Scholar Gipsy*."

Size *12–15ft. (4–5m.)*
Raiser *Mattock, U.K. 1973*
Parentage *Buccaneer x Arthur Bell*
Award *Gold Medal, Belfast*
Very fragrant

FREISINGER MORGENROTE *Page 91*

Synonyms: KORmarter; Morgenrote, Sunrise

The medium-sized double blooms are borne in clusters on plants of moderate growth. Grown in the raiser's display garden as a wide Shrub with arching sprays of spectacular proportions.

The soft orange blooms, heavily shaded copper-red, are sweetly scented. There are few good Climbers of this color, which explains its popularity. In the smaller garden, it will find a place growing on low walls, over arches and on pillars. Bronze-green, plentiful foliage.

Size *8ft. (2.5m.)*
Raiser *Kordes, Germany 1994*
Parentage *Lichkonigen Lucia x seedling*
Sweetly fragrant

GRAND HOTEL Page 103

Synonym: MACtel

A fine deep red Climber which continues to bloom throughout the summer and (in warm zones) fall. The double crimson blooms, enlivened by lighter shadings, are of good regular cup shape and grow in well-formed clusters on an upright plant, branching prolifically to make a fine display when trained on a fence. It tolerates a north-facing aspect. Of average height, Grand Hotel can be kept within bounds to make a neat shrub for the back of a mixed border. The bronze-green foliage is luxuriant.

Size *8–10ft. (2.5–3m.)*
Raiser McGredy, U.K. 1972
Parentage *Brilliant x Heidelberg*
Slight fragrance

HANDEL Page 104

Synonym: MACha

The small Hybid Tea-shaped buds are so neat that one often sees them used as boutonnières. The color can be variable, due to climatic change: strength of sunshine and temperature can both play a part. The buds are creamy white, splashed cherry pink to red, and as the blooms unfold, the shading spreads across the face of the opening flower, remaining deeper at the frilled petal edge.

An upright grower, clothed in dark green foliage, it carries the sprays of bloom continuously throughout the summer and even fall. Handel is suitable for growing on walls, fences, arches, and pillars. It can even be pruned to make an upright, mid-height shrub.

Size *8–10ft. (2.5–3m.)*
Raiser McGredy, U.K. 1965
Parentage *Columbine x Heidelberg*
Awards *TGC, RNRS; Gold Medal Portland, Oregon 1975; Award of Garden Merit, RHS*
Slight fragrance

JOSEPH'S COAT Page 96

A moderate grower which can also be treated as a Shrub rose. Joseph's Coat is, as its name implies, of many colors, showing that the old Floribunda rose Masquerade figures in its ancestry. Shades of golden-yellow, orange, and red appear on the wide-open petals of the semi-double blooms, borne in clusters, which open at different times, accentuating the color change.

To receive the full benefit from the spread of bloom when growing it as a Climber, train each branch as horizontally as possible, having fan-trained the bush from an early age.

Size *6–8ft. (2–2.5m.)*
Raiser Armstrong and Swim, U.S.A. 1964
Parentage *Buccaneer x Circus*
Awards *TGC, RNRS; Gold Medal Bagatelle, France 1964*
Slight fragrance

KING TUT Page 98

Synonym: CHEWarvel; Laura Ford

Patio climber. The elegant little buds are like miniature Hybrid Teas and of soft yellow with deeper gold shading, deepening as the opening flowers mature. The neatness of the bloom is reflected in the formation of the clusters, which can hold from five to ten blooms, and the plentiful, disease-resistant, light green foliage. An excellent choice to grow on a pillar or to fan-train on a trellis.

The size of the flowers, the foliage, and the neatness aand weather resistance of the blooms make this, the first of Chris Warner's patio climbers, a fine variety which will tolerate most aspects.

Size *8–10ft. (2.5–3m.)*
Raiser Warner, U.K. 1989
Parentage *(Anna Ford x Elizabeth of Glamis) x (Galway Bay x Sutter's Gold)*
Awards *Certificate of Merit, RNRS 1988; Award of Garden Merit, RHS*
Fragrant

MADAME ALFRED CARRIÈRE Page 95

One of the few Noisette roses still grown, it was described in 1908 as "the best white Climber." A large, vigorous grower, it can reach some 20ft. (6m.) and needs a lot of space, both vertically and horizontally when grown on a wall. Its thin, flexible shoots can, however, be trained easily over a pergola or fence.

The pale green, rather lightweight foliage is plentiful, as are the number of pale shoots, giving the undeserved impression of a weak grower, even though it is really vigorous and will tolerate the dappled shade of a northerly aspect. The full, globular blooms are pale creamy white with a hint of palest pink and with gold at the petal base, creating a pearl-like glow. They have the Tea fragrance of many older roses.

Size *up to 20ft. (6m.)*
Raiser *Schwartz, France 1879*
Award *Award of Garden Merit, RHS 1993*
Delightful Tea fragrance

MERMAID *Page 99*

A famous Old rose which will need careful siting in the smaller garden, as it can grow to 20ft. (6m.) and more—but, it can be cut back whenever it seems to be getting out of control. It is included here because there are many gardeners who feel that they must have the charm of Mermaid's single blooms and will create a space for it if they possibly can. These fragrant, 5–6in. (12–15cm.) sulfur yellow flowers open flat to reveal a tuft of stamens which remain an attraction even after the petals have fallen.

Mermaid has huge, hooked thorns ready to catch the unwary passerby—yet another reason for careful siting. The unique glossy foliage is another of this variety's characteristics.

Although recommended as tolerant of a northerly aspect, Mermaid may be cut back by extreme cold (though it will recover, as it is a robust grower). This late starter makes up for its tardiness by blooming, in some climes, well into fall.

Size *up to 20ft. (6m.)*
Raiser *Paul, U.K. 1918*
Parentage *R.bracteata x yellow Tea rose*
Awards *Gold Medal RNRS 1917; Award of Garden Merit, RHS 1993*
Very fragrant

PATIO QUEEN *Page 93*

Synonyms: CHEWsea; Nice Day

Patio climber. One of the most delightful of the small-flowered climbing miniatures. The perfect form of the glowing salmon pink blooms is greatly enhanced by a sweet fragrance. Borne in large, shapely clusters through summer and into autumn, the color may lose its brilliance if the plant is grown in the full glare of hot sun, but it is an obvious choice for dappled shade where the bloom and its color will last longer.

The glossy medium green foliage is lightly tinted copper-red when young and sets off the bloom in a particularly beautiful manner. The young plant may be shrubby but will mature into a true Climber, well worth waiting for.

Size *6–8ft. (2–2.5m.)*
Raiser *Warner, U.K. 1992*
Parentage *Seaspray x Warm Welcome*
Very fragrant

PENNY LANE *Page 103*

Synonym: HARdwell

The first Climbing rose to be selected Rose of the Year in the U.K., in 1998.

The palest pearl-blush or champagne-colored blooms, while being most elegantly modern in shape and prolificity, retain the charm of the Old rose varieties seen in flower paintings.

The delicate shades of soft pink found deep within the unfolding petals of the bloom are beautifully set off by the glossy, dark green foliage. Borne sometimes in wide clusters and at other times singly, the blooms are superb for cutting and have the substance to last.

Having slightly pliant stems, the plant is vigorous and, although it has been commercially available for only a season or two, has already found many admirers. It will tolerate dappled shade and is ideal for walls, fences, pergolas, arches, and pillars.

Size *8–10ft. (2.5–3m.)*
Raiser *Harkness, U.K. 1998*
Parentage *New Dawn x seedling*
Fragrant

RAMIRA *Page 102*

Synonyms: KORmeita; Agatha Christie

This is a vigorous grower to 8ft. (2.5m.) with heavy medium green glossy foliage. The large, soft pink Hybrid Tea-shaped buds open to full, fragrant, cupped blooms almost continuously from early summer to fall. The plant rejuvenates itself with much new growth from the base, at which point mature stems may be removed before becoming unsightly.

A useful Climber to grow fan shaped

on walls of most aspects, or on obelisks and pillars, it will make an attractive, rather loose-growing specimen shrub.
Size *8–10ft. (2.5–3m.)*
Raiser *Kordes, Germany 1990*
Fragrant

SPECTACULAR *Page 101*

Synonyms: Danse du Feu, Mada

One of the first of the Modern repeat-flowering Climbing roses. The oval buds are deepest red, opening to scarlet with orange-red shading before fading to leaden red. The blooms, produced over a long season, are borne in clusters set amid dark bronze-green glossy foliage. This hardy rose tolerates being planted in semi-shade but is prone to blackspot.
Size *8–10ft. (2.5–3m.)*
Raiser *Mallerin, France 1953*
Parentage *Paul's Scarlet Climber x seedling*
Fragrant

SUMMER WINE *Page 97*

Synonym: KORizont

A superb Climber in glowing coral and salmon pink shades. The semi-double flowers open to reveal a boss of red stamens, each tipped with golden anthers. As the bloom develops, the golden-orange reflections fade, leaving salmon pink shades, which are delightful in themselves. Summer Wine blooms into the fall if deadheaded, but if the last blooms of summer are left, the hips will color well and remain into the winter.

The vigorous grower is pliant enough to train in a fan shape or around pillars and obelisks. It is excellent for growing on large arches and tall tripods, where the blooms' sweet perfume is an added attraction.
Size *12–15ft. (4–5m.)*
Raiser *Kordes, Germany 1984*
Awards *TGC, RNRS; Award of Garden Merit, RHS*
Very fragrant

SWAN LAKE *Page 95*

Synonym: Schwanensee

Large, fragrant, well-shaped blooms of silvery pale pink are borne in clusters on long stems, making this a dual-purpose variety: it climbs well on walls of most aspects and is good on pillars, arches, and obelisks; and the long stems allow for cutting where the blooms are long lasting. It is most attractive in the fall, when the pale, ghostlike blooms are seen at their best in late afternoon.
Size *6–8ft. (2–2.5m.)*
Raiser *McGredy, U.K. 1968*
Parentage *Memoriam x Heidelberg*
Fragrant

TRADITION *Page 100*

Synonyms: KORkeltin; Tradition 95

A vigorous Climber with pliable growths, Tradition can be grown in place of the nonrepeating red Ramblers. The crimson-scarlet semi-double blooms are borne in enormous clusters throughout the summer and even into the fall.

Most prolific, it can be used to great effect on walls of all sizes, on fences, where it can be trained horizontally, on pergolas, and to clothe small buildings with its pliant growths. Tradition may be trimmed to shape, but it requires little or no pruning to promote regrowth and more bloom.
Size *12–15ft. (4–5m.)*
Raiser *Kordes, Germany 1995*
Fragrant

WARM WELCOME *Page 92*

Synonym: CHEWizz

Patio climber. Warm Welcome is unique among climbing miniatures. The fragrant, semi-double blooms are borne in clusters which clothe the plant from top to toe, colored tangerine-orange with orange-vermilion shadings, each petal has a golden zone at the base, enhancing the boss of stamens. The bronze-red juvenile foliage ages to deep green and is a perfect foil to the spectacular flowers borne on stems of deep plum-purple. The tall upright plant makes a superb pillar rose as well as being ideal for walls and arches.
Size *8–10ft. (2.5–3.5m.)*
Raiser *Warner, U.K. 1992*
Parentage *Elizabeth of Glamis x [(Galway Bay x Sutters Gold) x Anna Ford]*
Awards *PIT, RNRS 1988; Award of Garden Merit, RHS*
Fragrant

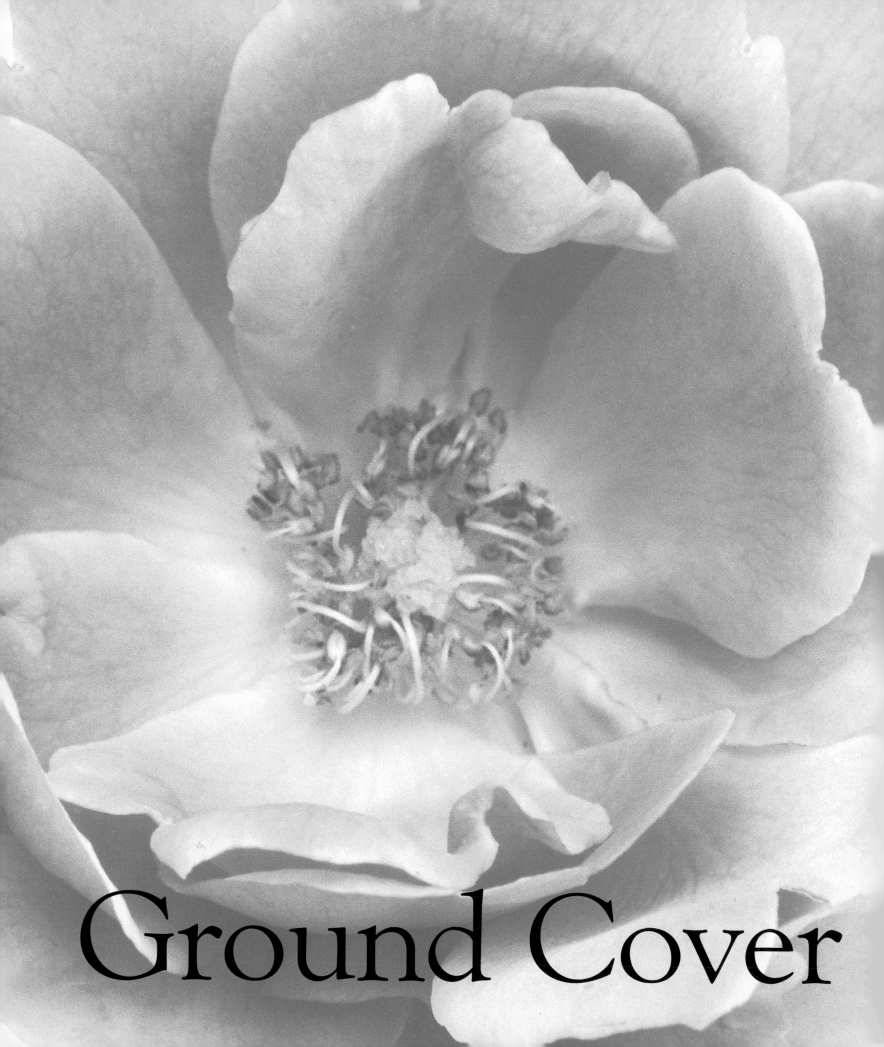

Ground Cover

WHITE FLOWER CARPET

One of today's most attractive white bedding roses.

FLOWER CARPET (PINK)

The disease resistance of this rose has earned it international acclaim.

PINK BASSIMO

A vigorous Ground Cover rose, whose light pink
blooms are set off by glossy, bright green foliage.

ROSELINA

The foliage and five-petaled single
flowers proclaim its *Rosa rugosa* ancestry.

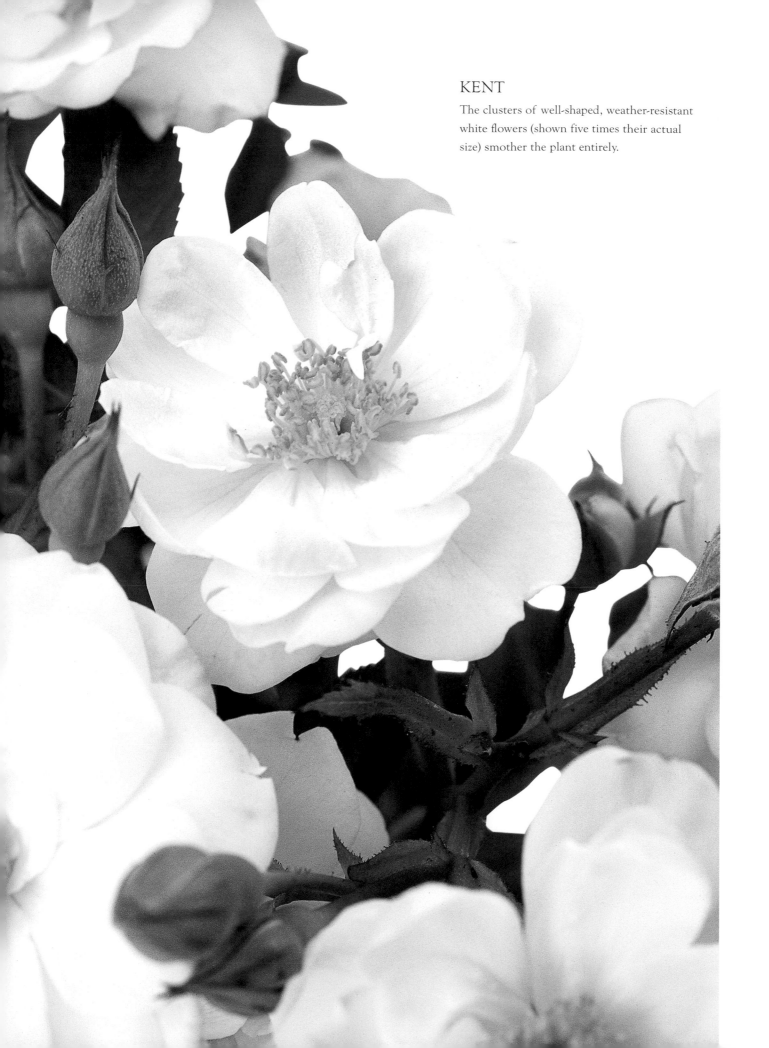

KENT

The clusters of well-shaped, weather-resistant white flowers (shown five times their actual size) smother the plant entirely.

ASPEN

A fine yellow Ground Cover rose with spreading growth (shown here twice its size).

SURREY

The best known of the County roses and one of the most versatile (shown four times its actual size).

SOMMERMÄRCHEN

A wide-spreading shrub amply clothed in shiny foliage (its actual size double that shown here).

THE FAIRY

This spreading, bushy grower (shown nearly twice its actual size) is an old favorite.

WILTSHIRE

Remains a mass of color even after the first frosts of autumn.

LANCASHIRE

An exceptional ground-hugging
plant in a rich, strong color.

BABY BLANKET

A robust grower, covering
the ground while
remaining very bushy.

Ground Cover roses

At one time some of the Shrub roses with a creeping, more sprawling habit were described as "ground cover roses," and these wide-spreading varieties, many of which had *Rosa wichurana* in their ancestry, were commonly used in roadside planting and park landscaping. Unfortunately most of them had inherited the once-only short season of flowering. The newer ground-hugging cultivars to which plant breeders turned their keen interest started to arrive only in the latter half of the twentieth century.

What makes these Ground Cover varieties such an asset to the smaller garden is that they grow to about 3ft. (90cm.) or so wide and they flower right through the seasons, from early summer until the first frosts bring the season to a close. Many of these roses are marketed in groups, such as the County Series, with the variety Surrey appearing in 1988, followed in the 1990s by the Flower Carpet Series, launched with a huge marketing campaign in Australia and Europe.

Ground Cover varieties make excellent subjects for borders and bedding and are very useful on banks, particularly where the ground is too steep for planting the more upright-growing roses. These roses also make excellent subjects for large planters and containers, where their spreading growth hangs over and softens the hard edges. The more prostrate varieties have also been used to great effect in hanging baskets, planting three or four plants in a basket 12–15in. (35–40cm.). Given careful cultivation—watering daily in the height of summer and adding a high-potash liquid feed weekly—a basket will last for two or three seasons before needing to be renewed.

ASPEN *page 115*

Synonyms: POULurt; Gold Magic Carpet, Gwent, Sun Cover

The cup-shaped double blooms are bright yellow when they first unfold, later becoming a soft cream, making an almost two-colored effect in maturity.

The spreading bush is less invasive than some of the Ground Cover varieties, and it is well covered in dark green, leathery foliage. It has been used to great effect in hanging baskets. Named 'Gwent' in Britain to celebrate holding the 1992 National Garden Festival in Ebbw Vale, Gwent, Wales, thus joining the County Series group.

Size *3ft. x 18in. (90 x 45cm.)*
Raiser *Poulsen, Denmark 1992*
Slight fragrance

BABY BLANKET *Page 119*

Synonyms: KORfullwind; Oxfordshire, Sommermorgen, Summer Morning

One of the best of the famous strain from Kordes of Germany, and winner of three well-deserved Gold Medals. The cup-shaped blooms of pale pink are borne in clusters on a vigorously bushy plant. Many of the petals show a likeness to other roses of the County Series, with frilled edges.

This superb ground-hugging variety is one of the most vigorous, clothed in bright green disease-resistant foliage.

Size *5 x 2ft. (150 x 60cm.)*
Raiser *Kordes, Germany 1991*

Awards *Gold Medal RNRS 1993; Gold Medal Coutrai; Gold Medal Monza*
Parentage *Surrey x seedling*
Lightly scented

THE FAIRY *page 117*

Synonyms: Fairy, Feerie

An attractive variety even when not in flower, which is useful because its season starts a few weeks after most other varieties. However, once it starts to bloom this delightful rose is smothered by layer upon layer of clusters of tiny rosette-shaped flowers of soft rose pink.

As with most repeat blooming shrubs, The Fairy can be kept within bounds and in shape by judicious pruning, which makes it suitable for many uses in the garden: as ground cover, as a hedge planted to tumble over a low bank or retaining wall, to fill a bed on a terrace, or as a subject for a large planter. It also makes a spectacular weeping standard.

Size *4 x 3ft. (120 x 90cm.)*
Raiser *Bentall, U.K. 1932*
Awards *Award of Garden Merit, RHS*
Little or no fragrance

FLOWER CARPET *page 112*

Synonyms: NOAtraum; Blooming Carpet, Emera, Enera Pavement, Heidetraum, Pink Flower Carpet

A good Ground Cover rose which has had many extravagant claims made for it. The color is a slightly crude, hard pink,

and it blooms somewhat later than most of this type. However it does not need deadheading, seeming indeed to thrive on neglect on this count. The leathery, dark green foliage is as disease-resistant as any rose can be, given the conditions under which it may find itself.

Size *3 x 2ft. (90 x 60cm.)*
Raiser *Noack, Germany 1989*
Parentage *Immensee (Partridge) x Amanda*
Awards *Gold Medal Glasgow; Award of Garden Merit, RHS; TGC, RNRS*
Slightly fragrant

KENT *page 114*

Synonyms: POULcov; Pyrenees, Sparkler, White Cover

Kent is one of the most useful ground-cover plants. It has been described as a dwarf spreading shrub, as a bedding Floribunda, and as a Ground Cover rose. Whichever classification you choose to place it under, a multitude of uses can be found for it. As a small shrub, it makes a handsome specimen among dwarf shrubs or as a highlight in bedding. As a bedding rose it is superb planted en masse. In the smaller garden it can, in fact, be successful anywhere, even grown as a low hedge.

The large clusters of pure white semi-double flowers are well-shaped, fitting nicely into the shrub's low, rounded outline. The flowers are most weather resistant and at the height of the season smother the plant to such an extent that little is seen of the foliage. Kent maintains this covering of blooms continuously, which makes it an excellent plant for every garden.

Size *2½ x 2½ft. (75 x 75cm.)*
Raiser *Poulsen, Denmark 1988*
Awards *PIT, RNRS 1990; Gold Medal, Baden Baden 1990; British Rose Award 1998*
Light fragrance

LANCASHIRE *Page 118*

Synonym: KORstegli

As is to be expected, the name 'Lancashire' must apply to a red rose, though in appearance this ground-hugging variety is quite different from that chosen by the House of Lancaster as its emblem during the English Wars of the Roses. The cherry-red double blooms are borne in shapely clusters in quick succession through summer and into the fall.

One of the County Series, Lancashire makes an excellent low-spreading ground cover. Its habit of growth also makes it a suitable container plant for trailing over the edge of large planters, as well as a good subject for hanging baskets. It makes a spectacular weeping standard too, flowering all through the season.

Size *3 x 2ft. (90 x 60cm.)*
Raiser *Kordes, Germany 1998*

PINK BASSIMO *Page 113*

Synonyms: KORbasren; St. Tiggywinkle

Another very vigorous Ground Cover rose, whose fresh, light pink blooms have a prominent white center, accentuating the boss of golden stamens. The blooms are borne in clusters continuously throughout the summer and into fall, and are beautifully set off by the luxurious, glossy bright green foliage. This ground-hugging shrub is an excellent subject for the smaller garden.

Size *4 x 3ft. (120 x 90cm.)*
Raiser *Kordes, Germany 1998*
Parentage *R.wichurana seedling x Robin Redbreast*
Award *Gold Medal 1992*
Light fragrance

ROSELINA *Page 113*

Synonyms: KORsaku; Playtime

A Ground Cover rose with a difference: the foliage, its prickles, and the appearance of the bloom all proclaim its *Rosa rugosa* origins. Unlike so many of the *R. rugosa* hybrids, however, it does not bear hips, and, as a result, flowers on and on. The single rose-pink five-petaled blooms are carried in clusters on a tough and healthy bush, which quickly forms a thicket; this makes it a superb plant for use in gardens of all sizes.

Size *3 x 3ft. (90 x 90cm.)*
Raiser *Kordes, Germany 1995*
Awards *TGC, RNRS; Crystal Prize Belfast 1995*

SOMMERMÄRCHEN *page 116*

Synonyms: KORpinka; Berkshire, Pink Sensation, Summer Fairy Tales, Xenia

A wide-spreading variety, becoming ever more popular as time goes by, hence the multitude of different names, which indicate that it is widely grown in many countries.

The large clusters of fragrant, well-shaped blooms open flat, as the brilliant deep cherry pink petals unfurl to reveal a prominent golden boss of stamens. They are borne on long, arching stems, clothed in glossy dark green foliage which is exceptionally disease resistant.

One of the first Ground Cover roses to bloom, it creates a blaze of rich color throughout the duration of the rose season. A truly excellent variety.

Size *4 x 2ft. (120 x 60cm.)*
Raiser *Kordes, Germany 1993*
Parentage *Weisse Immensee (Grouse) x seedling*
Awards *TGC, RNRS; Gold Medal Glasgow; Gold Medal Baden Baden; Gold Medal Geneva*
Fragrant

SURREY *Page 115*

Synonyms: KORlanum; Sommerwind, Vent d'Été

Somewhat taller than most of the famous County Series of ground-covering roses, Surrey is probably the most popular. It is an excellent choice for planting in large drifts in beds and borders and as specimen plants for smaller sites and in mixed shrub or perennial borders.

The soft pink, double cup-shaped blooms develop an attractive frilled edge as they unfurl. The blooms present a mass of pink, borne, as they are, in large trusses throughout the summer and well into fall.

Growing into a tall (if unpruned) and wide ground-hugging shrub, Surrey also makes a spectacular hedge, but would need careful siting in the smaller garden, where it could easily dominate.

Size *4 x 3ft. (120 x 90cm.)*
Raiser *Kordes, Germany 1988*
Parentage *The Fairy x seedling*
Awards *Gold Medal, RNRS 1987*
Slight fragrance

WHITE FLOWER CARPET

Page 111

Synonyms: NOAschnee; Emera Blanc, Opalia, Schneeflocke

One of the most attractive and popular low-growing white bedding roses available, on account of its neat, compact, ground-hugging habit. When it is fully established, the clusters of bloom can reach spectacular size and shape. The pure white blooms, large for the size of the bush, are saucer-shaped when mature, revealing the stamens in a pretty manner.

The compactness of the bush makes this an ideal variety to plant in small terrace beds and in containers, besides its obvious use in mass planting. The dark green, very glossy foliage adds to its obvious attractions.

Size *2 x 2ft. (60 x 60cm.)*
Raiser *Noack, Germany 1991*
Parentage *Immensee x Margaret Merrill*
Awards *Gold Medal, RNRS; Golden Rose of the Hague 1995; Certificate of Merit, Glasgow 1996*
Fragrant

WILTSHIRE   *Page 118*

Synonym: KORmuse

One of the longest flowering of the popular County Series. The spreading ground-hugging shrubs are a mass of bright pink even after the first frosts of autumn have decimated other garden flowers.

The semi-double blooms are borne in clusters and, because of continual re-growth, may give a layered effect as the new blooms overtake the maturing ones. The growth is sufficiently lax to make Wiltshire an ideal subject to grow where it can fall over a retaining wall or the edge of a large planter.

Size *3 x 2ft. (90 x 60cm.)*
Raiser *Kordes, Germany 1993*
Parentage *Partridge x seedling*
Awards *Certificate of Merit, RNRS; Certificate of Commendation, Glasgow*
Some fragrance

Shrub roses

CORNELIA

One of the most popular
Hybrid Musk roses
raised in the 1920s by the
Rev. Mr. Pemberton
(shown here three times
its actual size).

CÉCILE BRUNNER

The "sweetheart rose" is a dainty
jewel, half the size shown here.

GOLDEN WINGS

Thought by many to be the
most beautiful single rose.

TUMBLING WATERS

A small, spreading, sweetly scented shrub, ideal for a container on a terrace.

DE RESCHT
A fine Portland rose brought
back from Persia in the 1930s.

BALLERINA

Has large, rounded clusters of dainty dancing blooms, almost twice the size shown.

FRAU DAGMAR HASTRUP

A compact-growing hybrid of *Rosa rugosa*, with attractive hips.

JACQUES CARTIER

Brings the charm of the Old Rose garden
into the contemporary small space.

ROBUSTA

Vigorous, thorny, and repeat blooming,
Robusta makes a good
boundary hedge.

Shrub roses

Found under the headings of Old Garden roses, Species roses, and Modern Shrub roses, we find a bewildering array of rose varieties. Differentiated from bedding roses more by their habit of growth than by their breeding, Shrub roses may be defined as roses whose shape and outline allow them to be used as specimen plants, not necesssarily to grow among other subjects. They flower from quite low down on the plant, so that when viewed from the side—as opposed to looking down on the bloom, as with bedding roses—they appear to be covered in bloom from the ground upward.

Not all Shrub roses will fit into small gardens, but those shown here and elsewhere in the book can be accommodated in modest schemes, where their repeat blooming characteristic and their more restrained habit make them a decided asset. These Shrub roses, which may be loosely defined as rose bushes while not falling into the classes of bedding rose, may be used in mixed borders or hedges, and some may also be available as standards (Tree roses) because of

their neat, compact habit. By careful selection of varieties, even some of the Old roses (Shrub roses from previous centuries) may find a place in our smaller gardens. A few of the shorter-growing Moss roses, while only summer flowering, could be squeezed in, such as Nuits de Young. If you are aiming for the look of the old-fashioned rose, try some of the surviving Portland roses, such as Jacques Cartier and De Rescht. Portlands, with their full blooms and pastel colors, grow to less than 3ft. (90cm.) in height and flower throughout the summer and fall.

The individual entries make it clear which recognized category each profiled rose falls into. The new English roses, which also fall into the Shrub category, merit a section of their own and will be found on pages 136–145.

BALLERINA *Page 129*

The name of this splendid rose describes the dancing single blooms, with each light pink petal edged and shaded with a deeper hue. The flowers, borne in large, rounded clusters, are reminiscent of large-flowered hydrangeas. The elegant shrub is clothed to the ground in medium-green foliage.

This versatile variety can be used as a specimen on its own, in mixed borders of herbaceous and other plants, or in a Shrub rose border. Ballerina also makes a delightful hedge, blooming with a massive display at the start of the season and thereafter producing colorful sprays of flowers intermittently until another mass of bloom announces the arrival of autumn. Once the last blooms have finished, the shrub is sprinkled with a host of tiny jewel-like hips of bright amber and orange-red.

Classification *Modern Shrub rose, repeat blooming*
Size *3 x 3ft. (90 x 90cm.)*
Raiser *Bentall, U.K. 1937*
Award *Award of Garden Merit, RHS*
Slight fragrance

CÉCILE BRUNNER *Page 126*

Synonyms: Madame Cécile Brunner, Mignon, Sweetheart Rose, Maltese Rose

Perfectly formed, double, fragrant little blooms of china pink are borne in small sprays carried on almost thornless stems. They are often used in miniature floral arrangements at flower shows.

The dainty, low-growing bush is ideal for the front of a planting, whether in a rose bed or a mixed flower border. The foliage is small and, as with most China roses, tinted copper red when young. This is a famous old variety which has produced a tall, vigorous climbing sport. Care should be taken when purchasing this variety that it is the true small grower; some garden centers may be selling a more vigorous bush with similar flowers (Bloomfield Abundance) erroneously labeled Cécile Brunner.

Classification *China rose, Shrub rose, repeat blooming*
Size *2 x 2ft. (60 x 60cm.)*
Raiser *Ducher, France 1881*
Award *Award of Garden Merit, RHS*
Sweet fragrance

CORNELIA *Page 125*

One of the most popular of the Hybrid Musk roses bred in the 1920s by the Reverend Joseph Pemberton. The first was bred from Trier, a white variety with a superb scent from Lambert, in Germany. Others of Pemberton's roses include Felicia, Buff Beauty and Penelope, among others no longer listed.

The flowers of Cornelia are borne in sprays on cascading arched branches, which are thornless. The rosette-shaped blooms are of small to medium size, their color an attractive blend of apricot, salmon, orange, and strawberry pink. The fragrance has been described as "musky," referring to the deep sweet perfume, which is one of the most outstanding attractions of all the Hybrid Musks.

When in full flower, Cornelia is a remarkable beauty, clothed in dark bronze foliage which is lightly tinged red in its juvenile stages.

Classification *Modern Shrub rose, Hybrid Musk*
Size *4 x 4ft. (120 x 120cm.)*
Raiser *Pemberton, U.K. 1925*
Award *Award of Garden Merit, RHS*
Very fragrant

FRAU DAGMAR HASTRUP *Page 129*

Synonym: Frau Dagmar Hartopp

Did Mr. Hastrup name his masterpiece after his own wife (or relative) or after Mr. Hartopp's wife? The argument goes on but, whatever the story, his rose will live on for many years. It is an excellent variety which will readily find a home in many gardens, large and small. The neat, compact grower of manageable height is smothered in typically heavy wrinkled Rugosa foliage.

The large, soft, silvery pink single blooms are produced from late spring until fall, when they give way to a heavy crop of bright orange and red hips, beloved by birds, who will eventually strip the bush.

Frau Dagmar makes a superb low hedge and, as with most Rugosas, will sucker freely. If a budded specimen is planted the union should be below ground level.

This is a delightful, spectacular shrub especially when both flowers and fruit are borne at the same time.

Classification *Modern Shrub rose, Rugosa hybrid*
Size *3 x 3ft. (90 x 90cm.)*
Raiser *Hastrup, Denmark 1914*
Awarded *Award of Garden Merit, RHS*
Very fragrant

GOLDEN WINGS *Page 126*

A fine variety bred in the United States, this five-petaled scented rose of palest lemon yellow is quite large for a single rose. It opens to reveal dark stamens and, while it looks rather delicate, it is in fact both tough and weather resistant. The removal of spent flowerheads will ensure continuity of bloom throughout the summer and into the fall.

The vigorous, neat bush is prickly and twiggy, after the manner of its briar ancestry, and is both hardy and healthy, an ideal variety for the mixed border.

It has been said that the more involved rosarians become with their favorite flower, the more they appreciate the simplicity of the five-petaled rose. Never has this been more true than in the case of Golden Wings.

Classification *Modern Shrub rose, repeat flowering*
Size *4 x 4ft. (120 x 120cm.)*
Raiser *Shepherd, U.S.A. 1956*
Parentage *Soeur Thérèse x (Rosa pimpinelifolia Altaica x Ormiston Roy)*
Awards *Gold Medal ARS 1958; Award of Garden Merit, RHS*
Sweet fragrance

JACQUES CARTIER *Page 130*

Synonyms: Marchesa Boccella, Marquise Boccella

A fine variety of the Old Garden rose type, sufficiently short and compact to be accommodated in the smaller garden. Of upright habit, the growth is sturdy, and the blooms are borne in tight clusters over most of the summer and into fall.

The soft pink blooms are very full, and the inner petals are quartered and quilled to produce the shape so popular with the Victorians and characteristic of the Old Rose garden. Their fragrance is superb. The juvenile foliage is light green and develops a bluish tinge as it ages.

This is a great rose for bringing the past into our modern small garden; it will make a fine hedge as well as being suitable for the mixed border.

Classification *Old Garden rose, Portland rose*
Size *2ft. x 3½ft. (60cm. x 1.1m.)*
Raiser *Desprez, France 1842*
Very fragrant

DE RESCHT *Page 128*

A small, dense shrub bringing the charm of the Old Garden roses to the smaller garden, where its unusual color and its ability to bloom from early summer until well into fall makes it especially welcome.

The full double blooms are a rounded cushion shape of fuchsia purple petals surrounding a central button of incurved petals, tinted red and purple within the depths of the flower. The compact, rather upright, shrub is well furnished with dark green foliage. Overall it is an easy rose to place for lovers of Old roses with limited space at their disposal.

Classification *Old Garden rose, Portland rose*
Size *Up to 3ft. x 3ft. (90cm. x 90cm.)*
Introduced *into Europe by Miss Nancy Lindsay of Sutton Courtenay, Oxfordshire, from Rascht, Iran, in the late 1930s.*
Very fragrant

ROBUSTA *Page 131*

Synonym: KORgosa; Kordes' Robusta

A vigorous upright-growing Shrub rose which declares its *Rosa rugosa* ancestry by the mass of thorns that clothe all its stems.

The dark, almost blackish crimson slim buds open to large, single bright crimson blooms, revealing golden stamens. The well-shaped clusters are of good size and borne freely throughout the summer and into the fall.

Of an open habit, Robusta can grow quite tall and makes an excellent boundary hedge if pruned lightly, bearing in mind its thorniness. If pruned hard, it will remain a bush of medium height. The foliage is glossy dark green.

Classification *Modern Shrub rose, repeat blooming*
Size *6–7ft. x 6–7ft. (1.8–2m. x 1.8–2m.)*
Raiser *Kordes, Germany 1979*
Parentage Rosa rugosa x *seedling*
Award *Certificate of Merit, RNRS 1980*
Slight fragrance

TUMBLING WATERS Page 127

Synonym: POULtumb

A low-growing shrub, ideal for the smaller garden. At one time it was considered for classification as a bedding (Floribunda) rose, but it was certainly not prostrate enough to put among the Ground Cover roses, despite its name.

The pyramidal spikes of bloom are reminiscent of the *Saxifraga longifolia* hybrid 'Tumbling Waters', from which it gets its name. The semi-double white blooms open flat to expose the golden stamens. The clustered spikes are positioned at all angles, and the cushion-shaped plant is eminently suitable for growing in planters as well as at the front of beds and borders. It also makes an attractive small weeping standard.

Classification *Modern Shrub rose, repeat blooming*
Size *3 x 2ft. (90 x 60cm.)*
Raiser *Poulsen, Denmark 1997*
Sweetly scented

English roses

ENGLISH GARDEN

Good for cutting and a great
favorite among flower arrangers.

GEOFF HAMILTON

The color and fragrance of the cup-shaped quartered blooms surpass all expectations.

GRAHAM THOMAS

The first blooms in a real yellow, carried in large clusters on slender stems.

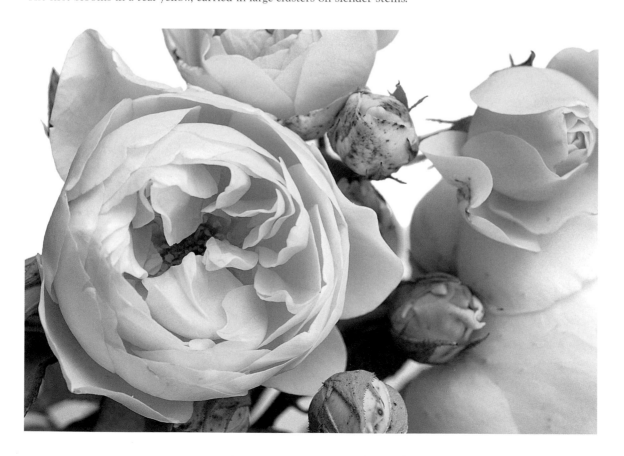

MARY ROSE

The large, full flowers, borne in rounded clusters, have a distinct damask fragrance.

THE PILGRIM

One of the most beautiful of the
English roses; its blooms have
curled and infolded small petals.

GOLDEN CELEBRATION
The large, cup-shaped, golden-yellow blooms
are a deeper golden-orange in the center.

EVELYN

The deep, exotic fragrance
of its full, heavy blooms
is enchanting.

English roses

Recent arrivals among the Shrub roses, the new English roses have been bred by David Austin to preserve the outstanding characteristics of the choice Old Garden roses and to give them the obvious virtues of modern hybridization and selection. These English roses are particularly remarkable for their fragrances, ranging from a delicate light fruitiness reminiscent of apples and lemons to the myrrh-like lushness of the old cabbage-rose Hybrid Perpetuals. In appearance, they capture the charm of the old Centifolias and Moss roses, as seen in the flower paintings of the Old Dutch Masters, and even the simplicity of the briar rose can be found in these modern masterpieces.

There are many different styles and heights of growth among the English roses, and care should be taken to make sure that the variety you choose is appropriate for your selected site.

ENGLISH GARDEN *Page 137*

Synonyms: AUSbuff; Schloss Glucksburg

Rather less of a shrub than most of the other English Roses from David Austin, English Garden is, in appearance, more akin to the large-flowered bedding rose. Its shape will therefore blend easily in a traditional bed of Hybrid Teas.

The creamy-buff blooms of beautiful shape open to large, flat flowers shot through with shades of harvest gold and apricot pink within the folds of the inner petals. They are ideal for cutting.

Size *2 x 3ft. (60 x 90cm.)*
Raiser *Austin, U.K. 1986*
Parentage *(Lilian Austin x seedling) x (Iceberg x Wife of Bath)*
Fragrant

EVELYN *Page 142*

Synonym: AUSsaucer

The large, full, many-petaled blooms are a beautiful soft tangerine buff shade, with apricot pink shading at the heart of the flower. The warmer the weather, the deeper the pink becomes, amid the folded and quilled petals. So heavy are these full blooms that the plant may require some support once the otherwise upright stem carrying several at a time causes the branch to arch.

The deep exotic fragrance is so gorgeous that this variety has been adopted by the firm of Crabtree & Evelyn, makers of traditional toiletries and perfume, to promote their products.

Size *2½ x 3ft. (75 x 90cm.)*
Raiser *Austin, U.K. 1992*
Parentage *Graham Thomas x Tamora*
Very fragrant

GEOFF HAMILTON *Page 138*

Synonym: AUSgold

Round cabbage-shaped buds open to glorious cupped blooms filled with swirls of folded petals. Lovers of Old Garden roses who appreciate how these flowers are portrayed in the old Dutch flower paintings will admire the way the delicately shaded outer petals frame the infolded, quartered blooms of light rose pink. The fragrance is all that one would expect of an Old rose. The blooms are borne throughout the summer and into the fall on strong, healthy shoots.

This rose is a great tribute to the late Geoff Hamilton, a British garden broadcaster on U.K. radio and television who had many admirers.

Size *5 x 5ft. (150 x 150cm.)*
Raiser *Austin, U.K. 1997*
Fragrant

GOLDEN CELEBRATION *Page 141*

Synonym: AUSgold

One of the few varieties with "gold" or "golden" in their name that really live up to the description. The fat buds of golden-yellow open to reveal a center made up of smaller petals in a deeper orange golden hue. The large, cup-shaped, very fragrant blooms may become so heavy in wet weather that some support is necessary.

This rounded bush of average size is a good subject for the mixed flower or shrub border, blooming throughout summer and into the fall.

Size *3 x 3ft. (90 x 90cm.)*
Raiser *Austin, U.K. 1992*
Parentage *Charles Austin x Abraham Darby*
Very fragrant

GRAHAM THOMAS *Page 138*

Synonyms: AUSmas; English Yellow, Graham Stuart Thomas

The first of David Austin's brilliant English roses in a real yellow. For some years aficionados had enjoyed Austin's pale pink and deep red shades and seen a few roses in orange buff tints, but the advent of Graham Thomas marked a major turning point in this series, owing much to the vogue for Old Garden rose look-alikes.

The deep golden buds open to fragrant cup-shaped blooms, revealing even deeper golden shades of a quality unusual in a rose and certainly never before seen in an Old Garden rose. Borne on long, slender stems, the blooms are in large clusters whose weight creates the typical arching habit.

A somewhat leggy plant, it is best planted in groups of three or five to make a clump, or it can be trained to form a restrained climber on walls or tripods with judicious pruning.

Named to honor the rosarian Graham Stuart Thomas, who has done much to popularize the revival of the Old Garden rose in Britain and elsewhere.

Size *2½ x 5ft. (75 x 150cm.)*
Raiser *Austin, U.K. 1983*
Parentage *Charles Austin x (Iceberg x seedling)*
Award *Award of Garden Merit, RHS 1993*
Fragrant

MARY ROSE *Page 139*

Synonym: AUSmary

The large, full flowers with a damask fragrance are borne in rounded clusters on arching branches. The color of this variety is variously described as "rich pink" or "strong rose-pink with a hint of lavender" and even "medium pink." The mature blooms shatter, rather than hanging on, which saves deadheading but is of no use to the flower arranger.

The round shrub is much branched and sturdy, the foliage medium green and disease resistant.

The rose was named in 1983 to celebrate the great marine archaeological feat of raising from the River Solent the "Mary Rose," the ill-fated flagship of Henry VIII's fleet.

Size *3 x 3ft. (90 x 90cm.)*
Raiser *Austin, U.K. 1983*
Parentage *The Friar x seedling*
Very fragrant

THE PILGRIM *Page 140*

Synonym: AUSwalker

This is one of the most beautiful of David Austin's English roses. A multitude of curled and infolded small petals arrange themselves in a most decorative manner in the heart of the quartered, flat bloom. The color ranges from tints of rich lemon in the center to the creamy yellow outer petals.

The well-shaped clusters of blooms are held on sturdy stems set amid the luxuriant medium green foliage. It can be planted to great effect in small groups or even as an individual specimen in a bed or border.

Size *3 x 5ft. (120 x 150cm.)*
Raiser *Austin, U.K. 1991*
Parentage *Graham Thomas x Yellow Button*
Fragrant

Care of roses

In spite of the stories that abound about the trouble roses can be, their cultivation is in fact quite simple. It is true that roses need good soil, but any soil (except an extremely acidic one, which roses do not like) can be enriched by the addition of rotted organic matter. Many of the ailments that were known to afflict roses, such as blackspot and mildew, are mostly a thing of the past now that disease resistance has been bred into modern varieties. Rose pruning is another task surrounded by myths which have deterred people from growing roses. In fact, trials have shown that a rose blooms as well after it has been drastically "pruned" by a hedge trimmer as when it has received lighter, more precise treatment with hand pruners. Feeding roses is a matter of common sense—a well-fed rose is a healthy plant which will flower well and is better able to resist disease. The essential guidelines to soil, planting, pruning, and avoiding pests and diseases are laid out very simply in the following pages.

Soil preparation

"Look over your garden wall with a beautiful rose in your coat, and your neighbour, loitering with his hands in his pockets, knee-deep in groundsel, amid his beds undrained and undug, will sigh from the depths of his divine despair, 'What a soil yours is for roses!'"

So wrote S. Reynolds Hole, the Dean of Rochester (England), in 1901. Dean Hole was one of the founders of the National Rose Society in 1876 (since the mid-twentieth century, the Royal National Rose Society) and is still a name to conjure with in the rose world. His story illustrates a popular misconception among gardeners, that roses need exceptional soil, dug three spits deep, and frequently enriched with quantities of organic matter, in order to thrive. The truth is that roses will grow in almost any soil, except an extremely acidic one, and in almost any country in the world. Certainly, if you live in a zone with extreme weather conditions, you will have to carry out extraordinary cultivations, but you should not experience difficulties in more temperate zones, provided that the soil is well prepared.

In establishing a garden, it is essential to know what type of soil you have. It would be wonderful if we all had the friable loam, rich in nutrients, associated with rose culture. However, the use of a good compost, or farmyard manure, is an excellent way of recycling natural materials to build up a healthy soil. It might be that yours is a thin, sandy, "hungry" soil, which will not retain moisture or nutrients, in which case a heavy dressing of farmyard manure, or the addition of well-rotted garden compost, and the use of an organic mulch, will help convert it to a state of fertility.

Your soil may, on the other hand, have the texture of heavy clay, which retains water and certainly makes digging more difficult. In this case you can add organic matter and gypsum or calcified seaweed to lighten the soil and to break down the clay by a process called flocculation. If one of the commercial preparations or sufficient lime is added to a clay soil, its tiny particles will form much larger "crumbs," enabling moisture and air to pass through more freely to the benefit of the plant rootlets. Organic manure, compost, or any other humus-making materials should be used regularly on all other kinds of soil, too, as a matter of routine.

The only soil roses will not grow in is a highly acidic soil, such as you find in areas noted for growing rhododendrons, azaleas, and winter-flowering heathers. You may come across the term "pH factor" here, the pH being the measurement of the soil's chemical composition, i.e. its degree of acidity or alkalinity. You can buy a soil testing kit from a garden center, or send a sample of soil to your local Extension Service, if you are unsure of your soil's chemical composition. If you find that your soil is highly acidic, you could still grow roses in containers, using a loam-based potting mix.

◄ The addition of organic matter will ensure a healthy rose that blooms well. Here, Climbing rose Madame Alfred Carrière helps to mask an unsightly shed, with hydrangea, euphorbias, and peonies.

▶ If you find your soil is acidic, you can still grow roses in loam-based potting mix in a container. Standard rose Loving Memory adds depth of color and becomes the focus of this collection of potted plants.

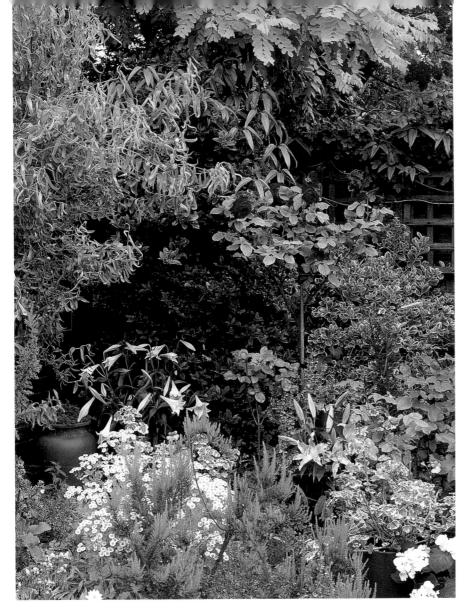

under "topsoil" to find a retailer who will have a source of good loam. If you have been unable to replace the infected soil, leave it for five years or so before introducing new roses to the same spot. There are preparations that claim to sterilize the soil, enabling one to forego soil replacement, but for a single rose, the effort and expense involved are not really worthwhile, and I have yet to be convinced that the process of chemical soil sterilization is completely effective.

Remember that a rose will last for a number of years, so dig the area well, removing all traces of perennial weeds, and incorporate a liberal dressing of well-rotted compost or farmyard manure. How deep you dig may depend on the structure of the soil's surface. Double-digging (i.e. two spade-depths), where possible, is most effective, but if your garden topsoil is only a spade's depth, that is how deep you should dig and manure. On no account should a gravel subsoil be disturbed and mixed in with your topsoil, and digging into heavy clay will only strain your back. Dried manure can be purchased in bags from a garden center, or if you have a source of rotted farmyard manure that has been stacked for at least six months, this is ideal. Horse, cow, or pig manure is best; poultry or sheep manure can be rather strong and burn young roots or shoots. Various other forms of organic matter, such as mushroom compost, cottonseed meal, or alfalfa meal, may be available at your garden center also.

Finally, before digging the planting hole, it is a good idea to make up a planting mixture to be worked into the soil at the bottom of the hole, and to sprinkle around the roots of the rose after planting it and before filling the hole with removed topsoil. Make up the mixture simply by adding two generous handfuls of sterilized bonemeal to a large bucket or small wheelbarrow load (say, 2½ gallons [10 liters]) of horticultural peat or one of the many alternatives. This will stimulate vigorous root action and give the rose an excellent start in its new home.

Having chosen the area of your garden where you wish to plant roses, you must then prepare the soil. If the proposed site has been occupied by a rose, or roses, within the last five years, it is imperative that the soil be replaced before planting. Remove at least a wheelbarrow load (say, 2 x 2 x 2ft. [60 x 60 x 60cm.]) of "old" soil and take it to another part of the garden not inhabited by roses and then replace it with fresh topsoil. This is because of a possible infection known as "rose sickness" or "specific rose transplant disease," which stays in the soil for several years after the removal of old, established roses. In small plots it is often difficult to find topsoil elsewhere in the garden to replace it with. If you need only a small quantity, a local garden center will almost certainly sell bags of topsoil, but where a large amount is required, look in the Yellow Pages

Planting roses

Marking out a rose bed

First decide on the effect you are aiming for, whether formal or informal, and prepare and clear the site. Then obtain a bunch of marking canes (2ft. [60cm.] tall) and a length of cord to mark out a straight planting line. Using the recommended planting distances (see right), work out the planting pattern and stick a cane in where each rose plant is to go. The front row should be parallel to the edge of the bed, leaving a 18in. (45cm.) border. Use the cord line to ensure straight lines if you want a formal bed. Make any necessary adjustments to achieve an overall sense of balance before starting to dig. Ensure that the soil is moist (but not wet) before digging the planting hole.

To plant a Shrub or bedding rose, follow the sequence shown opposite. If you have ordered bare-rooted roses and they arrive at an inconvenient time, or if the weather is too wet or too cold for planting, heel the roses in, temporarily planting them in a trench, where they may be safely kept until conditions improve.

Planting Climbing roses

When planting a climber against a wall or fence, take care to ensure that the site is not excessively dry, which is often the case when the wall is facing the sun. Prepare the ground thoroughly, then dig a planting hole at least 18in. (45cm.) away from the wall. Make the hole 2ft. (60cm.) square and deep enough to accommodate the roots or the rootball. At the bottom of the hole, incorporate a liberal dressing of organic planting mixture (see page 149). Place the plant in the hole as for a Shrub rose (see opposite), but with the cane leaning against the wall or fence. Keep the newly planted climbing rose well watered during the first season after planting. It is also advisable not to grow any other plants closer than 2ft. (60cm.).

Recommended planting distances

When planting new roses, check the ultimate height your plant is expected to reach in maturity. This will give you an indication of the recommended planting distance between like specimens, which should be about two-thirds of that height.

PATIO ROSES		18in. (45cm.) apart
HYBRID TEAS & FLORIBUNDAS		2ft. (60cm.) apart
SHRUB ROSES	Short	3ft. (90cm.) apart
	Medium	4ft. (1.2m.) apart
	Tall	6ft. (1.8m.) apart
CLIMBING ROSES		8ft. (2.5m.) apart minimum
STANDARD ROSES		4ft. (1.25m.) apart minimum

(Newly planted Hybrid Teas and Floribundas should be pruned hard in the first spring after planting, but newly planted Shrub roses and Climbing roses need no pruning in the first year.)

Planting a rose hedge

Prepare the site well, as for a rose bed (see page 148), and dig a trench along the line of the proposed hedge. The desired width of the hedge will restrict the choice of variety used. For a neat, upright hedge more than 3ft. (1m.) tall, a single line of upright (not bushy) Floribundas will be suitable. Should you want a thicker hedge, use a staggered line (i.e. two lines 6–12in. [15–30cm.] apart, with individual plants at alternate stations and no more than 2ft. [60cm.] between plants) to give the desired effect. Reduce the planting distances given above by at least 10 per cent for a hedge, as your aim is to present an unbroken line of growth.

1. Dig a hole large enough to accommodate the roots of a bare-rooted rose (this will be about the width and depth of the spade) or the rootball of a container-grown plant. At the bottom of the hole, fork up a tilth of loose, friable soil and and work in a handful of planting mix. Spread out the roots evenly in the planting hole.

2. Agitate the rose slightly to ensure that it is "sitting" comfortably in the planting mixture, then add another handful of planting mix and top up with removed soil, firming as you go. When planted, the point of union between the rootstock and the cultivar should be level with the surface of the soil.

3. Tread the soil round the plant to firm it in. This may need to be repeated after frosty weather and throughout the winter to prevent "wind rock." If planting a number of roses in a bed, it is a good idea to co-ordinate the procedure. After digging the hole and planting the first rose, fill the hole with soil removed from the next site, and so on.

Moving mature roses

It is unlikely that an ancient rose will survive being moved but, if a rose is less than five years old, you may wish to transfer it to a new site—or indeed a new garden—and care must be taken to ensure its survival. To dig out the old plant, first loosen it in the soil by cutting a circle around the base of the rose at a distance of 2–2½ft. (60–75cm.). You may need to do this in two stages—the first will loosen the compacted soil and the second time the spade, going in deeper, will sever the wide-spreading roots. Two people working at opposite sides will make the task easier. The soil making the rootball is not important and can be left behind.

Once the rose has been removed, prune the roots. Broken and scraped roots can be trimmed back cleanly, using a sharp knife or hand pruners. Remove any suckers you see, as well as snags of dead wood, and trim back very soft young shoots.

Soak the new site thoroughly before planting, especially if the weather has been dry (in which case it is also a good idea to moisten the roots before replanting). Once the wet soil starts to dry out, leaving the surround moist, plant your rose, using a planting mixture such as peat and bonemeal (see page 149). Firm in your replanted rose by treading down the infill with your foot. Keep a close eye on the replanted rose until it is re-established, watering at regular intervals if dry.

Pruning roses

Pruning roses involves the removal of aged, spent, or unsightly wood to promote healthy new growth in order to regenerate the plant. The purpose is to enable the rose to produce a good crop of blooms and foliage to grace the garden in the next season to follow.

It is worth observing a few basic rules to ensure success. Before starting to prune, tidy up the plant, not only to remove dead or diseased wood, but to make thing easier for you at the next stage. Weak or damaged shoots are extremely unlikely to produce good results. Aim to remove crossing shoots too, if possible, so that future growth will ensure that light and air can reach all parts of the plant; this will help to keep the foliage healthy. All cuts made should be finished cleanly, using an ultra-sharp pruning knife or a pair of hand pruners. Your sharp pruners will leave a clean, hygienic cut without ragged edges and ensure that the wound heals as quickly as possible. Make the cut on a slant, leaving the bud as near to the top of the remaining wood as possible, in order to leave no snags above developing new shoots. Stems should be cut back, leaving two or three buds on the previous year's growth.

Some authorities say that you must prune hard to be kind. Others say that if you do so, you are depriving the plant of its reserves by cutting back too far and that you need to reduce a bedding rose only by half to ensure good results. If a variety is tall and vigorous, with several thick, healthy stems growing from the base of the plant, these are the shoots that will produce fine blooms and strong, healthy foliage. If you want your garden to be a blaze of color, with masses of blooms in the early summer, light pruning to a third of last year's growth should produce the desired result. To achieve strong, healthy growth and foliage, together with blooms of good quality, harder pruning of last year's growth is acceptable. Whichever program you follow, it is essential to take note of the results and take them on board in future pruning regimes.

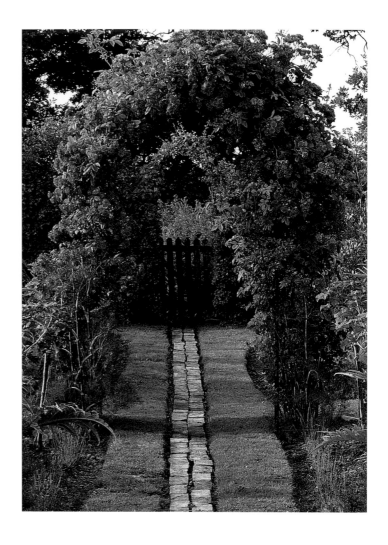

Pruning bedding roses

Hybrid Tea, Floribunda, patio, and Ground Cover roses are all varieties and types that flower on the current year's growth, and they should be pruned when the plants are dormant, if possible just before growth starts in early spring. If your rose is really old and has been pruned badly in the past, and the base of the plant is full of gnarled wood, you may need to carry out a drastic operation by cutting into the old, unsightly wood. Do so when the plant is almost completely dormant, i.e. midwinter. This will ensure that there is no sap rising in the plant and will therefore prevent any "bleeding" when you cut into it. You may need to use a saw

▲ This Rambler rose, swathing the arch, blooms on growth produced in the previous summer. It rejuvenates itself by regrowth from the base of the plant in late summer, so pruning should be carried out in early fall.

▲ The growth which has flowered may be cut back hard, leaving the new young growth to be tied in to replace it and to bear blooms the following summer. The form of a well-pruned rose can best be appreciated in winter.

recommended just before the onset of spring growth, the actual month or week depending on that year's weather pattern and your geographical location. If your roses are about to shoot into growth to about 2–3in. (5–8cm.), you have left it till just the right time to prune. Do not prune during periods of hard frost. This does not mean that the plant will be damaged by a "snap" frost the day after pruning, merely that the plant must not be frozen at the actual time of the cut. Iced tissue will bruise badly if touched at that time.

As we have seen under Planting Roses (page 150), newly planted bedding roses must be pruned hard (to about 4in. [10cm.]) in the spring after planting to ensure a good, broad-based framework on which the future of the plant will depend. The roots of your new plant will also be less stressed if they are not subjected to early spring winds.

Pruning Climbing roses

Almost all the recently introduced Climbing rose varieties bloom on the current year's growth. Therefore it does not greatly matter whether you prune hard or not, unless the plant has become top-heavy or if, after a few years, you wish to remove old or unsightly growth.

The main operation to which your Climbing rose needs to be subjected is training (see page 37). In most cases, the aim of training is to ensure that growth and therefore foliage and bloom are borne as close to the ground as possible. Tie all new and recently produced shoots down to an almost horizontal position. This means that you must have something to tie these branches to: use a wooden trellis, or fix wires to your wall or fence by means of masonry nails. If you are training your Climbing rose to a fan shape, you will see which shoots need shortening or removing. There will, of course, be some shoots that remain vertical. If, however, you try to hurry the coverage of the wall by training all shoots straight up, you will finish with a top-heavy plant with stems that are bare to about halfway up.

on the gnarled old wood. To the nervous gardener this may appear dangerous to the plant, but unsuspected dormant buds will be forced into growth by this drastic action. If such treatment does kill the rose—though it is unlikely—console yourself that the aged plant was no longer an ornament in the garden, and you have only hastened the inevitable.

At the end of the growing season, it is a good idea to trim your bedding roses back to a uniform height (say to 2ft. [60cm.] high). This will help to tidy up the garden for the winter and will stop "wind rock" in the taller specimens. Once the roots are exposed, they can easily be damaged by frost or by waterlogging. Early spring pruning is

1. Newly planted Hybrid Tea and Floribunda roses should be pruned the first spring after planting, before they start to produce shoots.

2. Fairly light pruning at this stage will allow your rose to produce some early blooms during its first year.

3. Harder pruning at the same stage ensures healthy basal shoots, better foliage, and large, shapely blooms in due course.

In the case of the older nonrepeating Climbing roses, the main frame of the plant should be left trained to cover the allotted area, while the lateral growths bearing blooms should be shortened to two or three buds in spring.

Ramblers, which also flower on growth made the previous year, need special treatment. They usually bloom profusely in midsummer and spend the rest of the growing season producing new growth from the base of the plant. Provided that this happens, all the summer's flowering growth can be removed by pruning after flowering and the new basal shoots should be securely tied in to bloom in the following season.

Pruning Shrub roses

Shrub roses also fall into two main categories: those that bloom on the previous year's growth and those that bloom on the current year's growth. The latter can easily be trimmed or pruned in order to shape the plant to fit the available space. It does not really matter if you cut these Shrub roses hard back—either way they will produce bloom in the forthcoming season. They may, however, lose the shape you have assiduously worked to produce. On the other hand, they will derive benefit from a severe trim. Take this opportunity to remove at the same time all dead, diseased, and straggly growth.

Shrub roses that bloom on the previous year's growth, which applies to most of the Old Garden roses, the Ramblers, the Species roses, and just a few of the Modern Shrub roses, would suffer seriously if you cut them hard back, and pruning hard at the wrong time would probably result in no bloom whatever in the following summer. Little or no pruning of the previous year's growth is required here; instead, the growths that have bloomed—and this usually means in midsummer, with no repeat in the fall—can be cut hard back in fall after flowering, provided you leave enough of the previous year's growth to bloom and enhance your garden the following year.

It is therefore essential to know exactly what roses you have and to which group they belong before embarking on your pruning program. If you move into a garden already stocked with roses and you do not know what type they are, seek help from a local horticulturist or garden center.

1. Standard roses require a certain amount of pruning after they have flowered.

2. Remove any spindly and/or diseased or dead wood before pruning the healthy, vigorous stems to a manageable length. Then stand back and observe—balance is particularly important with standard roses, and after pruning you may need to cut a little more to avoid lop-sided growth.

3. Harder pruning will produce better results in the long term, even if this means leaving just two or three buds on the remaining wood.

Pruning standard roses

Many Hybrid Tea and Floribunda varieties are also grown as standard (Tree) roses, and they need the selection of strong-growing shoots to encourage a well-balanced head, by means of careful pruning. Standard roses are budded onto rootstocks, the difference being that the budding takes place well above ground level. The stems of standards often produce suckers between the ground level and the "head" of the rose, and these should be rubbed off as soon as they appear. Do not allow them to ripen.

Pruning rose hedges

Pruning of the roses in a hedge is a little different from their treatment when grown in beds and borders. Especially where space is restricted, pruning needs to be done to achieve an even hedge of appropriate height and width, rather than pruning for maximum flower production. Hybrid Teas and Floribundas should be encouraged to regrow from the base of the plant each year. If you have not pruned down to a reasonable height, all regrowth will be from the top of the plants, and this may be repeated year after year. If this has occurred, and you wish to cut into old, gnarled wood, do so while the roses are dormant. Do not leave it until the onset of spring, or the wound will not heal properly and much sap and therefore vigor will be lost.

At the end of the flowering season, a hedge may be clipped to a uniform height, once you are not expecting any more blooms; by reducing the height, you will prevent wind-rock during winter gales. Do not allow a hedge to reach its intended height in one uninterrupted burst of growth; prune it down to the height of the lowest plant in the hedge in the early years. If your hedge is made up of Shrub roses, it may not need hard pruning, merely trimming to shape. Whether it is squared off or rounded at the edges is a matter of preference. If the Shrub roses are nonrepeating Old Garden types, they must never be pruned to produce bloom—to do so would make your rose hedge stay green throughout the year. Instead, lightly trim invasive shoots to a manageable length.

Repeat-flowering Shrub roses, i.e. varieties that bloom on the current year's growth, may be pruned to suit your requirements. Height may be achieved by light pruning, but if the hedge is becoming overcrowded, hard pruning will cause no harm. After a year or so of light pruning, mature Shrub roses, particularly Rugosas, may become bare at the base and will benefit from a hard prune in midwinter to restore them to the production of compact growth.

Feeding roses

The most important part of rose cultivation is to make sure your plants stay healthy by following good gardening practice. An organic approach, which is a way of working with nature, rather than against it, is recommended here, and as part of this regime, feeding, mulching, and good hygiene all play a crucial part. Healthy plants will flower well and are better able to resist most forms of pest and disease.

There are seven main elements that are essential to plant growth: nitrogen, phosphorus, sulfur, potassium, calcium, magnesium, and iron, in addition to what are commonly known as trace elements. An analysis of your soil should show any particular deficiency. Organic fertilizers or feed (as opposed to inorganic chemicals) are readily available at garden centers. One of the best compound feeds is a mixture of dried blood, fish meal and bonemeal: fish meal contains nitrogen and phosphates; bonemeal contains phosphate fertilizers for activating root action; and dried blood contains fast-acting nitrogen. Scatter a small handful around each rose as soon as the first leaves appear in the spring, and repeat this at the height of the main flowering. This second application should keep the plant in good health for the rest of the season. Alternatives include seaweed, which includes a complete range of trace elements, and dried animal manures, which are rich in humus-building nutrients.

It is also a good idea to spread an organic mulch, such as pulverized tree bark, around your roses to retain moisture in the soil. Not only will it smother annual weeds but it will aid the roses' assimilation of plant foods, even at the height of summer. Otherwise the soil would dry out, locking up most of the nutrients the rose needs in order to continue to produce strong, healthy growth, foliage, and blooms.

▸ *Well-fed Rambling roses The Garland (left) and Dorothy Perkins, together with Félicitté Perpétue (right), clothe the garden arches seen here in high summer.*

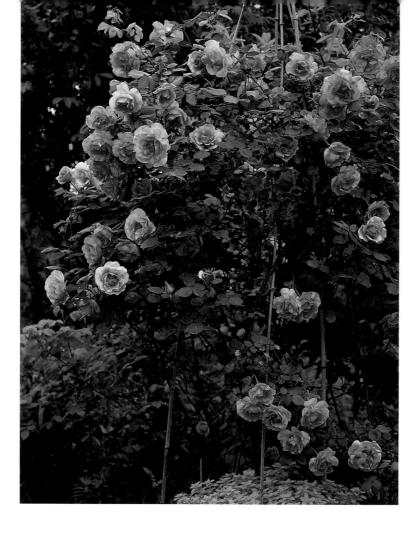

Keeping roses healthy

▲ A healthy, well-fed rose should stay free of attack by pests and disease. Climbing rose Bantry Bay, trained up a wigwam of canes, responds with a mass of blooms and shiny green foliage.

A well-grown and well-nurtured rose will be able to resist pests and diseases, whereas an unhealthy, starved plant will be the first to succumb. Apart from generous feeding (see page 156), there are some aspects of rose cultivation that you should follow to prevent particular problems.

Leaf shedding in midsummer

One of the commonest causes of leaf drop is lack of moisture and sustenance. Feed your roses with a balanced rose food, available from most garden centers, and mulch with organic compost and/or pulverized bark. This will retain moisture in the soil and help the plant roots draw up nutrients.

Lack of late-summer blooms

After the midsummer flush, repeat-flowering roses need a little extra cosseting, in the form of mulching and deadheading, to continue to perform well. The removal of spent blooms will stop seedheads (hips) from forming and taking the nourishment from autumn blooms. This applies to repeat blooming Hybrid Teas, Floribundas, and Climbers. Shrub roses prized for their production of ornamental hips should not, of course, be deadheaded. A few Ground Cover roses, particularly those with single flowers, will produce colorful hips if not deadheaded in summer; otherwise, they will bloom until very late in the season.

Discolored leaves

The foliage on a strong, healthy, well-nourished rose should be richly colored and mirror the plant's well-being. Discolored leaves give the first warning that all is not well. The chart opposite shows symptoms affecting foliage, their diagnosis, and recommended treatment. Leaves affected by blackspot should be picked off as soon as they are detected, then burnt, which should stop the attack spreading. Remove and burn all twiggy growths, together with any prunings.

Rose pests and diseases

A number of insect predators, such as ladybugs, attack and eat greenfly (aphids), the most common rose pest, though badly infected plants can also be sprayed with insecticidal soaps. Roses may become infected with fungal diseases in years when these are prevalent. To a great degree, these can be circumvented by keeping your plants strong and healthy through regular feeding and mulching, especially in early and late summer.

Dealing with weeds

The whole range of weed-killing potions, paints, and sprays currently for sale at garden centers and hardware stores all carry dire warnings about their misuse, which make it obvious that in the smaller garden the safest and best course of action is prevention. When preparing a new site for planting, it is imperative that all perennial weed roots be dug out and destroyed. Thereafter, mulches make admirable suppressants for annual weeds. The use of pulverized bark, applied in a 2in. (5cm.) layer over the top of the soil in between your roses, will control most annual weeds, and the occasional weed that escapes these attentions can easily be dealt with by hoeing or by hand weeding.

Symptom	Probable cause	What to do
Yellowing leaves	Lack of available iron (this even occurs in some iron-rich soils – the key word is "available")	Apply chelated iron in the form of sequestered iron.
Yellowing of leaf-tissue around veins	Magnesium deficiency	Water in ¾oz. (20g.) per sq. yd. (sq. m.) of Epsom Salts.
Pale green leaves	Lack of nitrogen	Apply a nitrogen-rich fertilizer.
Small leaves with reddish purple shading	Lack of phosphorus	Water in ¾oz. (20g.) of superphosphate.
Red/purple edges to leaves/brilliant red shading on juvenile growth	Lack of potash	Water in ¾oz. (20g.) sulfate of potash.
White deposit coating the leaves	Mildew	Spray with a good fungicide, and feed well until midsummer.
Round black spots (not purple) on green leaves or on leaves that have turned yellow in fall	Blackspot	As above, and pick off affected leaves and destroy. Feed well the following spring.

A layer of moss or green algae on the soil may point toward poor drainage, causing waterlogging, compaction of the soil, or a manurial deficiency. Hoeing, the use of an organic mulch, and feeding should take care of a minor problem, but serious drainage problems call for more drastic measures, which may involve laying trenches. However, most waterlogging is caused by abnormal weather conditions.

Removing suckers

Most roses are budded onto a rootstock. At one time most of the rootstocks were a form of dog rose (*Rosa canina*), a vigorous and often invasive wild rose. The vigor of the plant is what the propagator is using to the advantage of the cultivar. Selections of other rootstocks have sometimes been made on various grounds, such as incompatibility or a reduced likelihood of producing suckers.

Suckers are shoots that grow from the rootstock or from just below the bud union of the named variety (cultivar) and the rootstock. These growths can impede the rose's performance. Tracing the suspect shoot to its origin is often the most reliable way to identify a sucker. An old tale, often repeated through ignorance, is that the number of leaflets on a bract is a sure sign of identity. The truth is that modern varieties are so mixed up in their ancestry that the inherited number of leaflets is immaterial and can vary even on the same plant, so the number of leaflets may be the same on a sucker as on the cultivar. Compare the rogue shoot with the juvenile as well as the mature growth of a budded shoot; if it is the same or similar, it is probably not a sucker.

A rose may be induced to sucker if it has been damaged by hoeing too near the root, or by wrongly hacking off a previous sucker at ground level, leaving a stump to grow again. Planting a new specimen too loosely also encourages suckering. Deal with a sucker as soon as you see it: follow the course of the shoot in question, which may involve moving soil away until you discover its origin. Then pull off the sucker, wearing suitable gloves. If you cut a sucker, you may only be pruning it, which encourages renewed vigor.

Roses for special purposes

Although roses fall into various groups based on a worldwide classification, it is often more helpful to see them listed according to their use in the garden. The following lists include all the roses which feature in this book (marked with an asterisk*); they are based on, but do not rigorously follow, the lists of Roses of Special Merit published by The Royal National Rose Society, the world authority on roses.

Key to headings and abbreviations:

Name Varietal name used in reference lists

Code International code for identification of variety and raiser (the first three letters are those of the breeder's name). Where no code name is given, this rose predated the practice of giving international names.

Height The heights given are for mature plants grown under average conditions of cultivation and under different and/or particular circumstances may vary from the norm.
S short: 18in.–2ft. 6in. (45–75cm.); M medium: 2ft. 6in.–3ft. (75–100cm.);
T tall: 3ft. (1m.) upward

Fragrance F barely perceptible fragrance, FF fragrant, FFF very fragrant

Climbers W: for walls & fences P: for pillars & obelisks A: for arches & pergolas

ROSES FOR MIXED BEDS AND BORDERS

Name	Code	Height	Type	Color	Fragrance
Amber Queen	HARroony	S	Fl	Amber-yellow	FF
Anna Livia*	KORmetter	M	Fl	Rose-pink	F
Aspen*	POULurt	S	GC	Lemon-yellow	F
Avon	POULmulti	S	GC	Pale blush	F
Baby Blanket*	KORfullwind	M	GC	Soft pink	F
Ballerina*		M	Sh	Pale pink	F
Belle Epoque	FRYaboo	M	HT	Amber/bronze	FF
Comte de Chambord		M	Sh	Pink	FFF
Congratulations*	KORlift	T	Fl	Soft pink	F
Cornelia		M	Sh	Pink	FFF
Crystal Palace*	POULrek	S	Pat	Creamy peach	F
Dawn Chorus*	DICqueen	M	HT	Tangerine-orange	FF
Elina	DICjana	T	HT	Primrose-yellow	FF
English Garden*	AUSbuff	T	Sh	Soft apricot-yellow	FF
Evelyn*	AUSsaucer	M	Sh	Apricot	FFF
Felicia		T	Sh	Shaded pink	FFF
Festival*	KORdialo	S	Pat	Crimson scarlet/silver	F
Flower Carpet*	NOAtrum	M	GC	Deep pink	F
Fredensborg*	POULmax	S	Fl	Shrimp-pink	F
Freedom	DICjem	M	HT	Chrome-yellow	F
Geoff Hamilton*	AUSham	M	Sh	Shades of pink	FF
Gertrude Jekyll	AUSbord	T	Sh	Deep pink	FFF
Golden Celebration*	AUSgold	M	Sh	Deep gold	FFF
Golden Wings*		M	Sh	Pale lemon-yellow	FF
Graham Thomas*	AUSmas	T	Sh	Rich yellow	FFF
Hannah Gordon*	KORweiso	M	Fl	Shaded pink	F
Hansaland	KORhassi	T	Sh	Crimson scarlet	F
Heritage	AUSblush	T	Sh	Shell-pink	FFF
Hertfordshire	KORtenay	S	GC	Carmine-pink	F
Iceberg*	KORbin	T	Fl	White	FF
Ice Cream	KORzuri	M	HT	White shaded ivory	FF
Ingrid Bergman*	POULman	M	HT	Glowing dark red	FF
Irish Eyes	DICwitness	S	Fl	Yellow and scarlet	F
Jacques Cartier*		S	Sh	Warm pink	FFF
Just Joey*		M	HT	Apricot-buff	FF
Kent*	POULcov	S	GC	White	F
L.D. Braithwaite	AUScrim	T	Sh	Deep crimson	FFF

Name	Code	Height	Type	Color	Fragrance
L'Aimant	HARzola	T	Fl	Coral-pink	FFF
Lancashire*	KORstegli	S	GC	Crimson	FF
Lavaglut*	KORlech	M	Fl	Deepest crimson	F
Little Bo-Peep	POULlen	S	Pat	Palest pink	F
Livin' Easy*	HARwelcome	M	Fl	Deep orange	F
Mandarin*	KORcelin	S	Pat	Orange and pink	F
Many Happy Returns	HARwanted	M	Fl	Silvery pink	F
Mariandel*	KORpeahn	M	Fl	Deep crimson	F
Mary Rose*	AUSmary	T	Sh	Rose pink	FFF
Molineux	AUSmol	T	Sh	Rich yellow	FFF
Oranges and Lemons*	MACanlorem	T	Fl	Yellow striped orange	F
Paul Shirville	HARqueterwife	M	HT	Peach, salmon shading	FFF
Peace*		T	HT	Yellow, pink shading	F
Peace of Vereenigen*	KORverpea	T	HT	Scarlet/gold reverse	F
Pink Bassimo*	KORbasren	S	GC	Glowing pink/white eye	F
Playtime*	KORsaku	M	GC	Pink	F
Queen Mother*	KORquemu	S	Pat	Soft pink	F
Remember Me	COCdestin	M	HT	Coppery orange	F
De Rescht*		M	Sh	Fuchsia-purple	FFF
Royal William*	KORzaun	T	HT	Deep crimson	FF
Sally Holmes		T	Sh	Ivory shaded buff	FF
Selfridges*	KORpriwa	T	HT	Bright yellow	FF
Sharifa Asma*	AUSreef	M	Sh	Blush pink	FFF
Shocking Blue*	KORblue	M	Fl	Rich lilac-magenta	FFF
Silver Jubilee*		M	HT	Apricot-salmon	F
Sommermarchen*	KORpinka	M	GC	Cherry pink	F
Sunset Boulevard*	HARbabble	M	Fl	Orange apricot	F
Sunsprite*	KORresia	M	Fl	Brilliant yellow	FFF
Surrey*	KORlanum	M	GC	Soft rose-pink	F
Sweet Dream*	FRYminicot	M	Pat	Creamy apricot	FF
Tequila Sunrise*	DICobey	S	HT	Yellow shaded red	F
The Fairy*		M	GC	Soft rose-pink	
The Pilgrim*	AUSwalker	T	SH	Pale lemon-yellow	FFF
Trumpeter*	MACtrum	S	Fl	Glowing scarlet	F
Tumbling Waters*	POULtumb	M	Sh	White	FF
Tynwald*	MATwyt	T	HT	Ivory white	FF
Valencia*	KOReklia	T	HT	Buff-orange	FFF
Warm Wishes	FRYxotic	M	HT	Salmon-peach	F
Whire Flower Carpet*	NOASchnee	S	GC	White	FF
Wiltshire*	KORmuse	S	GC	Bright rose-pink	F
Winchester Cathedral	AUScat	M	Sh	White	FFF
Worcestershire	KORlalon	M	GC	Lemon-yellow	F

ROSES FOR HEDGES

Name	Code	Height	Type	Color	Fragrance
Alexander	HARlex	T	HT	Scarlet	
Ballerina*		M	Sh	Pale rose	F
Cornelia		M	Sh	Pink shades	FFF
Frau Dagmar Hastrup*		M	Sh	Silver pink	FF
Golden Wings*		M	Sh	Pale lemon	FF
Hansaland	KORhassi	T	Sh	Crimson-scarlet	F
Iceberg	KORbin	M	Fl	White	FF
Jacqueline du Pré	HARwanna	M	Sh	White	FF
Kent*	POULcov	S	GC/Sh	White	F
Korresia*	KORresia	S	Fl	Bright yellow	FFF
L.D. Braithwaite	AUScrim	M	Sh	Deep crimson	FFF
Little Bo-Peep	POULlen	vS	Pat	Palest pink	FF
Mariandel*	KORpeahn	S	Fl	Rich crimson	F

Name	Code	Height	Type	Color	Fragrance
Mary Rose*	AUSmary	M	Sh	Rose-pink	FF
Robusta*	KORgosa	T	Sh	Crimson	F
Romantic Hedgerose	KORworm	M	Fl	Pink	F
R.rugosa 'Alba'		M	Sh	White	FFF
R.rugosa 'Rubra'		M	Sh	Rose-pink	FFF
R. rubrifolia*		T	Sh	Rose-pink	F
De Rescht*		S	Sh	Fuchsia-purple	FFF
Roselina*	KORsaku	S	GC	Pink	F
Surrey*	KORlanum	M	GC	Soft pink	F
The Fairy*		S	GC/Sh	Soft pink	
The Pilgrim*	AUSwalker	M	Sh	Pale lemon	FFF
Winchester Cathedral	AUScat	M	Sh	White	FF

Name	Code	Type	Color	Fragrance
Graham Thomas*	AUSmas	WP	Golden-yellow	FFF
Grand Hotel*		WPA	Bright crimson	F
Handel*	MACha	WPA	White shaded pink	F
Joseph's Coat*		P	Yellow/orange	F
Laura Ford*	CHEWarvel	WPA	Golden-yellow	FF
Little Rambler*	CHEWramb	PA	Palest pink	FFF
Mermaid*		W	Primrose-yellow	FF
Madame A. Carriere*		W	Pearly white	FFF
New Dawn		WPA	Flesh-pink	FF
Nice Day*	CHEWsea	WPA	Salmon-pink	FFF
Open Arms*	CHEWpixcel	PA	Light pink	F
Penny Lane*	HARdwell	WPA	Champagne	FF
Ramira*	KORmeita	W	Soft pink	FF
Spectacular*		W	Cinnabar-red	F
Summer Wine*	KORizont	WA	Coral-pink	FFF
Sunrise*	KORmarter	PA	Yellow and orange	FFF
Swan Lake*		WPA	Palest pink	FF
Sympathie		WPA	Scarlet	F
Tradition*	KORkettin	WPA	Crimson	FF
Warm Welcome*	CHEWizz	PA	Orange-vermilion	FF
White Cloud	KORstacha	W	Creamy white	FFF

ROSES FOR WALLS & FENCES (W) , PILLARS (P), PERGOLAS & ARCHES (A)

(All roses listed would tolerate a northern or easterly aspect)

Name	Code	Type	Color	Fragrance
Altissimo*	DELmar	WP	Crimson-scarlet	F
Bantry Bay		WPA	Soft pink	F
Compassion*		WPA	Pink shaded apricot	FFF
Dreaming Spires*		WP	Golden-yellow	FFF
Golden Showers		WPA	Clear yellow	F

Color schemes for roses

There exists a range of popular color schemes involving roses, co-ordinated and not, and the following lists may help planning your beds and borders as well as walls, fences, and patio containers. The suggestions given are not intended as hard and fast rules but simply as a guide to the range of roses you may choose after deciding on a color scheme for your garden. They can be referred to when planning a rose-only bed, to avoid color clashes, and may be used in conjunction with your choice of companion plants (see pages 46–9).

Vermilion and scarlet
Bedding Alexander, Fragrant Cloud, Livin' Easy, Peace of Vereenigen, Trumpeter, St. Boniface, Top Marks
Climbing Climbing Orange Spectacular, Sunblaze, Sympathie

Orange and yellow
Bedding Amber Queen, Belle Epoque, Dawn Chorus, Fellowship, Freedom, Irish Eyes, Just Joey, Korresia, Mandarin, Molineux, Peace, Remember Me, Selfridges, Tequila Sunrise
Patio containers Aspen, Irish Eyes, Mandarin
Borders Golden Celebration, Golden Wings, Graham Thomas, Gwent, Molineux, Oranges and Lemons, Peace, Selfridges
Climbing Dreaming Spires, Freisinger Morgenrote, Golden Showers, Golden Celebration, Graham Thomas, Joseph's Coat, King Tut, Warm Welcome

Yellow and gold
Bedding Amber Queen, Aspen, Elina, Freedom, Just Joey, Molineux, Selfridges, Sunsprite
Patio containers Aspen, Worcestershire
Borders Golden Celebration, Golden Wings, Graham Thomas, Peace, Selfridges, The Pilgrim, Worcestershire
Climbing Graham Thomas, Golden Celebration, Golden Showers, King Tut, The Pilgrim

Apricot and gold
Bedding Belle Epoque, Crystal Palace, Dawn Chorus, Elina, English Garden, Evelyn, Just Joey, Sunset Boulevard, Sweet Dream
Borders Buff Beauty

Peaches and cream
Bedding Crystal Palace, Elina, English Garden, Evelyn, Paul Shirville, Sunset Boulevard, Sweet Dream
Borders English Garden, Evelyn, Sally Holmes
Climbing Penny Lane, Compassion, Schoolgirl

White
Bedding Avon, Elina, Iceberg, Kent, Memoire, Tumbling Waters, White Flower Carpet, White Pet
Borders Iceberg, Jacqueline du Pré, Kent, White Flower Carpet, Winchester Cathedral, R. rugosa alba
Patio containers Avon, Kent, Little White Pet, Tumbling Waters, White Flower Carpet
Climbing Baby Rambler, Penny Lane, White Cloud, Swan Lake

White and pink
Bedding Anna Livia, Avon, Congratulations, Geoff Hamilton, Hannah Gordon, Iceberg, Many Happy Returns, Queen Mother, Roselina, Silver Jubilee, The Fairy, White Flower Carpet, Winchester Cathedral
Borders Ballerina, Comte de Chambord, Congratulations, Felicia, Geoff Hamilton, Heritage, Pink Bassimo, Roselina, Sharifa Asma, Winchester Cathedral, Frau Dagmar Hastrup, R. rugosa 'Alba', R. rugosa 'Rubra'
Patio containers Avon, Natchez, Pink Hit, Queen Mother, The Fairy, White Flower Carpet
Climbing Baby Rambler, Bantry Bay, Compassion, Graham Thomas, Handel, Open Arms, Patio Queen, Penny Lane, Ramira, Swan Lake, New Dawn

Shades of pink
Bedding Anna Livia, Baby Blanket, Ballerina, Comte de Chambord, Congratulations, Flower Carpet, Fredensborg, Geoff Hamilton, Hertfordshire, L'Aimant, Many Happy Returns, Mary Rose, Playtime, Queen Mother, Silver Jubilee, The Fairy, Wiltshire
Borders Baby Blanket, Ballerina, Berkshire, Comte de Chambord, Congratulations, Cornelia, Felicia, Flower Carpet, Geoff Hamilton, Gertrude Jekyll, Jacques Cartier, Mary Rose, Sharifa Asma, Surrey, The Fairy, Wiltshire, Frau Dagmar Hastrup, R. rugosa 'Rubra'
Climbing Bantry Bay, Compassion, New Dawn, Open Arms, Patio Queen, Ramira, Summer Wine

Pink and red
Bedding Anne Livia, Congratulations, Flower Carpet, Festival, Ingrid Bergman, Intrigue, Mariandel, Mary Rose, Royal William, Sommermarchen, Surrey, Trumpeter, Wiltshire
Borders Berkshire, Felicia, Cornelia, Hansaland, Robusta, Mary Rose, Surrey, Wiltshire
Climbing Altissimo, Bantry Bay, Grand Hotel, Ramira, Sympathie, Tradition

Crimson
Bedding Festival, Ingrid Bergman, Intrigue, Lancashire, Mariandel, Royal William, Suffolk
Borders L.D. Braithwaite, Hansaland, Lancashire, Robusta, De Rescht, Suffolk
Climbing Altissimo, Grand Hotel, Sympathie, Tradition

Rose suppliers

Many garden centers stock a good selection of roses. If they do not have the variety you want, ask to see a copy of The Combined Rose List, a 224-page book published each year since 1980. It contains essential information about more than 13,000 rose varieties, with mail-order sources in the US and Canada. Compiled and edited by Beverly R. Dobson and Peter Schneider, the book is available from Peter Schneider, Box 677, Mantua, Ohio 44255, U.S.A.

The American Rose Society
P.O. Box 30000
Shreveport
Louisiana 71130

The Antique Rose Emporium
9300 Lueckemeyer Road
Brenham
TX 77833-6453
Tel. (409) 836-9051
E-mail:
tandj@amityheritageroses.com,
www.amityhritageroses.com

Arena Rose Company
P.O. Box 3096
Paso Robles
CA 93447
Tel. (805) 227-4094
E-mail: www.arenarose.com

B & B Nursery & Propagators
2578 County Road I
Willows
CA 95988
Tel. (916) 934-2676

Bay Laurel Nursery
2500 El Camino Real,
Atascadero
CA 93422
Tel. (805) 466-3406

The Roseraie at Bayfields
P.O. Box R
Waldoboro
ME 04572
Tel. (207) 832-6330

Bear Creek Gardens, Inc.,
P.O. Box 9100
Medford
OR 975501-9899
Tel. (541) 770-2645

Bray's Rose Branch
15272 White Creek Avenue
Cedar Springs
MI 49319
Tel. (616) 696-8647

Carroll Gardens
444 East Main Street
Westminster
MD 21157
Tel. (410) 848-5422

Chamblee's Rose Nursery
10926 U.S. Hwy 69 North
Tyler
TX 75706-8742
Tel. 1-8000-256-7673
E-mail: roses@tyler.net,
www.chambleeroses.com

Dominion Seed House
P.O. Box 2500
Georgetown
Ontario L7G 5L6
Canada
Tel. (905) 873-3037
E-mail: www.dominion-seed
house.com

Edmund's Roses
6235 S.W. Kahle Road
Wilsonville
OR 97070
Tel. (503) 682-1476

The Fragrant Rose Company
Island Sun Greenhouses
8185 Island Highway
R.R. 1 Site 19-8
Fanny Bay
B.C. VOR 1WO Canada
Tel. (250) 335-2101

Garden Valley Ranch Nursery
498 Pepper Road
Petaluma
CA 94952
Tel. (707) 795-0919
E-mail: bareroot@gardenvalley.com,
www.gardenvalley.com

Cecil Goodman
4874 Lorece Avenue
Memphis
TN 38117
Tel. (901) 683-7950

Hand Rose Farms
113312 CR 433 Harvey Road
Tyler
TX 75706
Tel. (903) 882-7165

Heirloom Old Garden Roses
24062 Riverside Drive N.E.
St. Paul
OR 97137
Tel. (503) 538-1576

Hole's Greenhouses & Gardens Limited,
101 Bellerose Drive
St Albert
Alberta T8N 8N8
Canada
Tel. (403) 419-6800

Hortico Inc.
723 Robson Road
R.R. 1 Waterdown
Ontario LOR 2H1
Canada
Tel. (905) 689-6984

Howerton Rose Nursery
1656 Weaverville Road
Allen Township
Northampton
PA 18067
Tel. (610) 262-5412

Humber Nurseries Ltd.
R.R. 8 Brampton
Ontario L6T 3Y7
Canada
Tel. (905) 794-0555
E-mail: humber@gardencentre.com,
www.gardencentre.com

Jackson & Perkins Co.

One Rose Lane

Medford

OR 97501-0702

Tel. 1-800-872-7673

E-mail: www.jacksonandperkins.com

J.W. Jung Seed Co.

335 South High Street

Randolph

WI 53957-0001

Tel. 1-800-1297-3123

Sam Kedem Greenhouse and Nursery

12414 191st Street E.

Hastings

MN 55033

Tel. (651) 437-7516

Martin & Kraus

1191 Centre Road

P.O. Box 12

Carlisle

Ontario LOR 1HO

Canada

Tel. (905) 689-0230

E-mail: sales@gardenrose.com,

www.gardenrose.com

Michael's Premier Roses

9759 Elder Creek Drive

Sacramento

CA 95829

Tel. (916) 369-7673

E-mail: michael@michaelsrose.com,

www.michaelsrose.com

Sequoia Nursery

Moore Miniature Roses

2519 East Noble Avenue

Visalia

CA 93292

Tel. (209) 732-0190

Mori Miniatures

Box 7872

Virgil

Ontario LOS 1TO

Canada

Tel. (905) 468-7271

Mother Earth's

2300 Washington

Conway

AR 72032

Tel. (501) 450-7722

North Creek Farm

24 Sebasco Road

Phippsburg

ME 04562

Tel. (207) 389-1341

Old Mill Nursery

806 South Belt Highway

st Joseph

MO 64507

Tel. 1-800-344-8107

Oregon Miniature Roses, Inc.

8285 S.W. 185th Avenue

Beaverton

OR 97007-6712

Tel. (503) 649-4482

Carl Pallek & Son Nurseries

Box 137

Virgil

Ontario LOS 1TO

Canada

Tel. (905) 468-7262

Petaluma Rose Co.

P.O. Box 750953

Petaluma

CA 94975

Tel. (707) 769-8862

E-mail: proseco@aol.com,

www.sonic.net

Pickering Nurseries, Inc.

670 Kingston Road

Pickering

Ontario L1V 1A6

Canada

Tel. (905) 839-2111

Regan Nursery

4268 Decoto Road

Fremont

CA 94555

Tel. (510) 797-3222

Rose Fire Ltd

09 394 State Route 34

Edon

OH 43518

The Rose Ranch

P.O. Box 326

La Grange

CA 95329

Tel. (209) 8522-9220

Roses Unlimited

Route 1

Box 587

North Deerwood Drive

Laurens

SC 29360

Tel. (864) 682-7673

E-mail: roseunlmt@aol.com

Russian River Rose Company

1685 Magnolia Drive

Healdsburg

CA 95448

Tel. (707) 433-7455

Spring Valley Roses

N7637 – 330th Street

P.O. Box 7

Spring Valley

WI 54767

Tel. (715) 778-4481

E-mail: svroses@win.bright.net,

www.springvalleyroses.com

Stanek's

2929 East 27th Avenue

Spokane

WA 99223-4916

Tel. (509) 535-2939

Sylvan Nursery

848 Stonybrook Road

Kelowna

B.C. V1W 4P3

Canada

Tel. (250) 764-4517

Teas Nursery Co., Inc.

4400 Bellaire Boulevard

P.O. Box 1603

Bellaire

TX 77402-1603

Tel. (713) 664-4400

E-mail: teas@teasnursery.com,

www.teasnursery.com

Vintage Gardens

2833 Old Gravestein Hwy. South

Sebastopol

CA 95472

Tel. (707) 829-2035

E-mail: wwwspiderweb.com/vintage

Witherspoon Rose Culture

P.O. Box 52489

Durham

NC 27717-2489

Tel. (919) 489-4446

E-mail: roseswrc@aol.com,

www.netmar.com

Index of rose names

Index

Author's acknowledgments

Mark Mattock wishes to thank the following:

Mattocks Roses division of Notcutts Nurseries for supplying specimen blooms; Linda Burgess whose personal style of photography ensured that the evocative flower portraits add great originality to this book; Finest English Conservatories whose showhouses at Notcutts Garden Centre at Nuneham Courtenay provided excellent studio facilities for photography; James Mattock and Debbie Godfrey whose expertise on word processing and computers provided admirable support; members of the rose growing confraternity, including Angela Pawsey (editor of Find that Rose) and Ken Grapes (Director General of the Royal National Rose Society) whose interest and enthusiasm have encouraged the writing of this book. And, last but by no means least, all at Quadrille who have been involved with seeing the book through from its inception to its production with understanding and kindness.

Picture credits

The publisher thanks the photographers and agencies for their kind permission to reproduce the following photographs in this book:

2 Le Scanff-Mayer (Pépinère Delbard à Malicorne); 6 A Bouquet of Roses by Eugene Henri Cauchois (1850-1911) Private Collection/Bridgeman Art Library; 9 Royal Horticultural Society, Lindley Library; 10 Adelia aurclianensis, engraved by Victor, from 'Choix des Plus Belles Fleurs', 1827 (coloured engraving) by Pierre-Joseph Redouté (1759-1840) (after) Private Collection /Bridgeman Art Library; 12 Royal Horticultural Society, Lindley Library; 15 The Art Archive/Victoria & Albert Museum, London; 18 Simon McBride/Interior Archive (Garden: Jan Morgan); 20 Jerry Harpur (Designer: Diana Ross, London); 21 Jerry Harpur (Designer: Lisette Pleasance, London); 22 left Saxon Holt; 22-23 centre Simon McBride/Interior Archive (Garden: Hawkes); 23 above right John Glover; 24 left Andrew Lawson; 24-5 Andrew Lawson (Designer: Penelope Hobhouse); 26 left Nicola Browne (Designer: Gilles Clement); 26-27 Brigitte Thomas/GPL; 28 left Marcus Harpur (The Vine, Essex); 28 right Clive Nichols (Designer: Roger Platts); 29 Andrew Lawson (Designer: Wendy Lauderdale); 30 Le Scanff-Mayer (Le Jardin d'Anne-Marie (91) Lardy, France); 31 John Glover; 32 left Nicola Browne; 32 right Densey Clyne/GPL; 33 Clive Nichols (Meadow Plants, Berks); 34 left John Glover; 34-35 Ron Sutherland/GPL; 36 Jerry Harpur (Designer: Diana Ross, London); 37 Saxon Holt; 38 Clive Nichols (Designer: Sarah Raven–Daily Telegraph/American Express Garden, Chelsea Flower Show 1998); 39 Clive Nichols (Lower Hall, Shrops); 40 Marcus Harpur (Designer: Penelope Hobhouse); 41 Andrew Lawson; 42-43 Jerry Harpur (Designers: Janowski & Tokstad, San Francisco, CA); 44 Andrew Lawson (Designer: Penelope Hobhouse); 45 John Glover (Chelsea Flower Show, 1994); 46-7 Dency Kane (Designer: Brooks Garcia); 48 John Glover (Parham Park); 49 above Le Scanff-Mayer (Pépinère Delbard à Malicorne); 49 below Karen Bussolini; 148-149 Simon McBride/Interior Archive (Garden: Jan Morgan); 152-3 S&O Mathews; 156-7 S&O Mathews; 158 Le Scanff-Mayer (Jardin de Guy Thenot);

All other photographs were specially taken by Linda Burgess for Quadrille Publishing Limited.